CW00530253

LIVERPOOL

CLASSIC KITS

Whereas there was a time when people only bought football shirts to play football in, in the modern era fans want shirts to wear at matches and on non-matchdays to demonstrate their support. Fans throughout the world love to sport the proud red of Liverpool, a club with a fantastic history and a special place in the hearts of their global fan-base.

Liverpool's Classic Kits traces the strips the men from Anfield have worn over the last five decades telling the stories of the kits themselves and the seasons they were worn in. Home kits, change kits and even third choice kits are all featured with an array of facts and figures about the seasons featured. Any Liverpool fan will find Classic Kits a fascinating wander into the wardrobe of strips worn by the likes of Mo Salah, Steven Gerrard, Ian Rush, Kenny Dalglish and a host of top stars proud to have worn the shirt of one of the planet's most successful and glamorous football clubs.

Rob Mason

AUTHOR BIOGRAPHY

Rob Mason first saw Liverpool play in 1970. He has written 60 football books including Liverpool's Magnificent Number 7s and updated The Little Book of Liverpool as well as producing a biography of Jordan Henderson.

In 2015 he worked with LFC's official historian to erect a headstone in Anfield cemetery to mark the grave of Tom Watson, the manager of Liverpool's first ever league champions.

HO

ME

1977-78 HOME

Unlike in modern times, when if a kit lasts for two seasons it has unusual longevity, back in 1977-78 Liverpool's strip – like those of other teams – did not change much from season to season. Often if there was a difference, it was a subtle one rather than a radical departure as is sometimes seen in the 21st century.

CLASSIC VINTAGE KIT

As Liverpool took to the pitch as European champions in 1977-78, they did so in classic style. Shirts were not yet emblazoned with sponsors names or competition sleeve patches. Kenny Dalglish and co therefore wore a simple, red long-sleeved shirt with a white V-necked collar and white cuffs. A gold liver bird above the letters L.F.C. was only accompanied by a small and discreet gold Umbro logo on the other side of the shirt.

For the European Cup final against Brugge, when a Dalglish goal retained the trophy, the shirts that were worn had some additional gold embroidery under the club badge. This simply read, 'European Cup Final, Wembley 1978'. In that year's League Cup final against newly-promoted Nottingham Forest, Liverpool wore their white away kit at Wembley, taking to the pitch in matching white tracksuit tops. In the replay at Old Trafford, though, it was Liverpool's turn to wear their home kit and so they donned their famous red shirts matched with the usual plain all-red shorts and socks.

Losing the talismanic Kevin Keegan after winning the European Cup for the first time in 1977 left most supporters feeling bereft. However the genius that was Bob Paisley replaced Special K with an even more special player and banked £60,000 difference into the bargain; £440,000 of the £500,000 received for Keegan made its way to Celtic in exchange for Kenny Dalglish, arguably the finest footballer to ever pull on a Liverpool jersey.

Dalglish didn't take long to settle in – seven minutes to be precise! That's how long it took him to score on his league debut at Middlesbrough. On the opposite side that day at Ayresome Park was Graeme Souness, another Scot who by the end of the season would provide the pass from which King Kenny would be crowned as he scored the only goal of the European Cup final against Club Brugge at Wembley. They were joined by a third great Scot in Alan Hansen. 22-year-old Hansen had arrived late the previous season in a £100,000 deal from Partick Thistle. Although he only played in 26 games in his first full season of 1977-78, Hansen would go on to be as important at the back as Virgil van Dijk is in the modern day, just as Dalglish and Souness were every bit as influential as Mo Salah and Jordan Henderson are more than four decades on.

Shortly before Christmas in 1977 Keegan made an emotional return to Anfield, playing for Hamburg in the European Super Cup. He had also played in the first leg which had been drawn 1-1 in Germany but, like his teammates, was swept away on Merseyside as, incredibly, Keegan's side were humiliated 6-0. It was Kevin's successor Kenny who put the cherry on top of the cake with the final goal.

As well as the two European trophies, Liverpool also claimed a share of the Charity Shield after a goalless season curtain-raiser with Manchester United at Wembley. In between then and the European Cup final there was another trip to beneath the old twin towers in the League Cup final. On that occasion Liverpool played in their white away kit against Nottingham Forest but, after a goalless draw, donned their red shirts in the replay at Old Trafford which was lost 1-0 to a controversial penalty. Brian Clough's Forest also took the League Title, deposing Liverpool as champions. It was a disappointment for the Anfielders, who finished as runners-up, but at least the ultimate honour was once again in the Liverpool trophy room for a second magnificent season.

RUNNERS-UP

No first-half goals were conceded in the opening 10 league games.

3RD ROUND

4-2 home win for Chelsea.

RUNNERS-UP

John Robertson scored the winner in the replay for Forest.

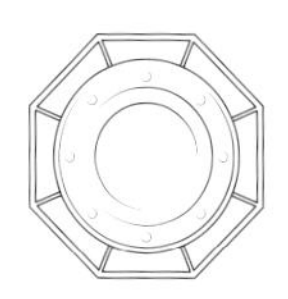

WINNERS

82,000 packed into Wembley to see the final.

WINNERS

Liverpool became the first British team to retain the European Cup.

WINNERS

McDermott hat-trick winning it for Liverpool.

AVERAGE HOME LEAGUE ATTENDANCE

45,546

HIGHEST ATTENDANCE
51,668 VS EVERTON

LOWEST ATTENDANCE
38,249 VS QPR

BOB PAISLEY

KENNY DALGLISH

21 Ray Clemence kept more clean sheets in the league than Dalglish scored goals: 21 in 40 games.

Steve Ogrizovic also kept a clean sheet in one of his two appearances.

The European Cup final saw Ian Callaghan on the bench in his last game.

The season was also the final one for hard-man Tommy Smith.

46 Benfica had gone 46 games without defeat when Liverpool beat them in the European Cup quarter-final.

1982-83 HOME

Liverpool's home shirts had been a simple, plain red ever since they proudly sported the colour for the first time on the 1st of September 1896, having changed from the blue and white worn in their first season.

PLAIN RED WITH PINSTRIPES

This iconic shirt was worn in March of 1983, in the League Cup final against Manchester United (as pictured) as Liverpool once more secured silverware under legendary manager Bob Paisley. For the 1982-83 season, in which the club's second shirt sponsor Crown Paints replaced Hitachi, the red shirt of Liverpool began to feature faint thin gold pinstripes, with the club badge and Umbro manufacturer's emblem also picked out in gold. The V-necked collar was white and red and a white stripe was also introduced on the side of the shorts, with white detailing featuring the shape of the Umbro logo at the top of the socks too. Once introduced this became the Liverpool home kit for three seasons until the end of 1984-85.

4-4-2 formations are often regarded as old-fashioned, even dinosaur-like in the 2020s, but back in the early eighties a rarely changed Liverpool line-up slotted into their 4-4-2 shape with devastating effect. The League Title was won in a canter, the Reds finishing nine points clear of runners-up Watford despite, astonishingly, taking just a single point from the final six games.

Bruce Grobbelaar commanded his penalty area behind a back four of Phil Neal, Mark Lawrenson (Phil Thompson until December), Alan Hansen and Alan Kennedy. The midfield engine room usually consisted of livewire Craig Johnston and enforcer/enabler Graeme Souness, with Sammy Lee and Glenn Whelan in the wide positions, while up front Ian Rush and Kenny Dalglish reigned supreme. Dalglish won both the Players' Player of the Year and Football Writers' Player of the Year awards.

Legendary manager Bob Paisley retired at the end of the season after delivering the sixth League Title in his nine years in charge. Paisley's was a golden era that brought innumerable cups, with this 1982-83 season bringing the Charity Shield as well as the League Cup for a third successive season. A hard-fought final saw Liverpool trail to Manchester United for over an hour before storming back to win in extra-time, Ronnie Whelan hitting the winner. What made this victory even sweeter than winning their third successive League Cup, was that it meant their bitter rivals fell short of their own historic marker. Had Manchester United won the League Cup as well as the FA Cup that year, they would have become the first team ever to have won the two competitions in the same season. Instead 100,000 fans at Wembley saw the Reds of Liverpool take home the silverware.

WINNERS

The League Title was won for a record 14th time.

5TH ROUND

2-1 away win for Brighton ended Liverpool's FA Cup run.

WINNERS

The League Cup was won for the third successive season, beating Manchester United.

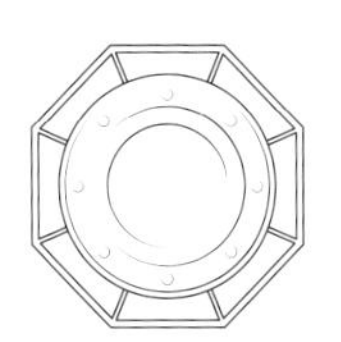

WINNERS

A 1-0 Wembley victory over Spurs.

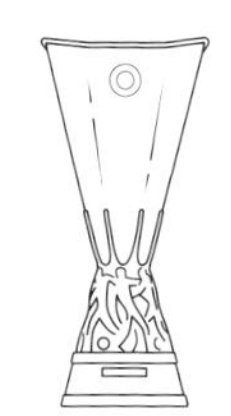

QTR-FINALS

Dundalk attracted the lowest gate of the campaign - 12,021.

BOB PAISLEY

IAN RUSH

AVERAGE HOME LEAGUE ATTENDANCE 34,834

HIGHEST ATTENDANCE
44,868 VS BRIGHTON

LOWEST ATTENDANCE
12,021 VS DUNDALK

60 Goalkeeper Bruce Grobbelaar and full-backs Phil Neal and Alan Kennedy played in all 60 games.

5 Five goals were scored six times: in 5-0 league wins over Southampton and Everton, 5-2 v Manchester City and 5-1 v Notts County and Stoke City, as well as 5-0 against HJK Helsinki in the European Cup.

44 Manager Bob Paisley retired at the end of the season after 44 years at the club and having been manager since 1974.

Liverpool lost 5 of their last 7 league games and drew the other two, yet they finished the season eleven points ahead of the second-placed Watford.

1985-86 HOME

This was a new era of Adidas kits for Liverpool. Following a spell wearing Umbro apparel the team first sported the Adidas kit – minus the Crown paints sponsorship – in the ill-fated European Cup final in May 1985 on the night of the Heysel tragedy.

FIRST TIME WITH ADIDAS

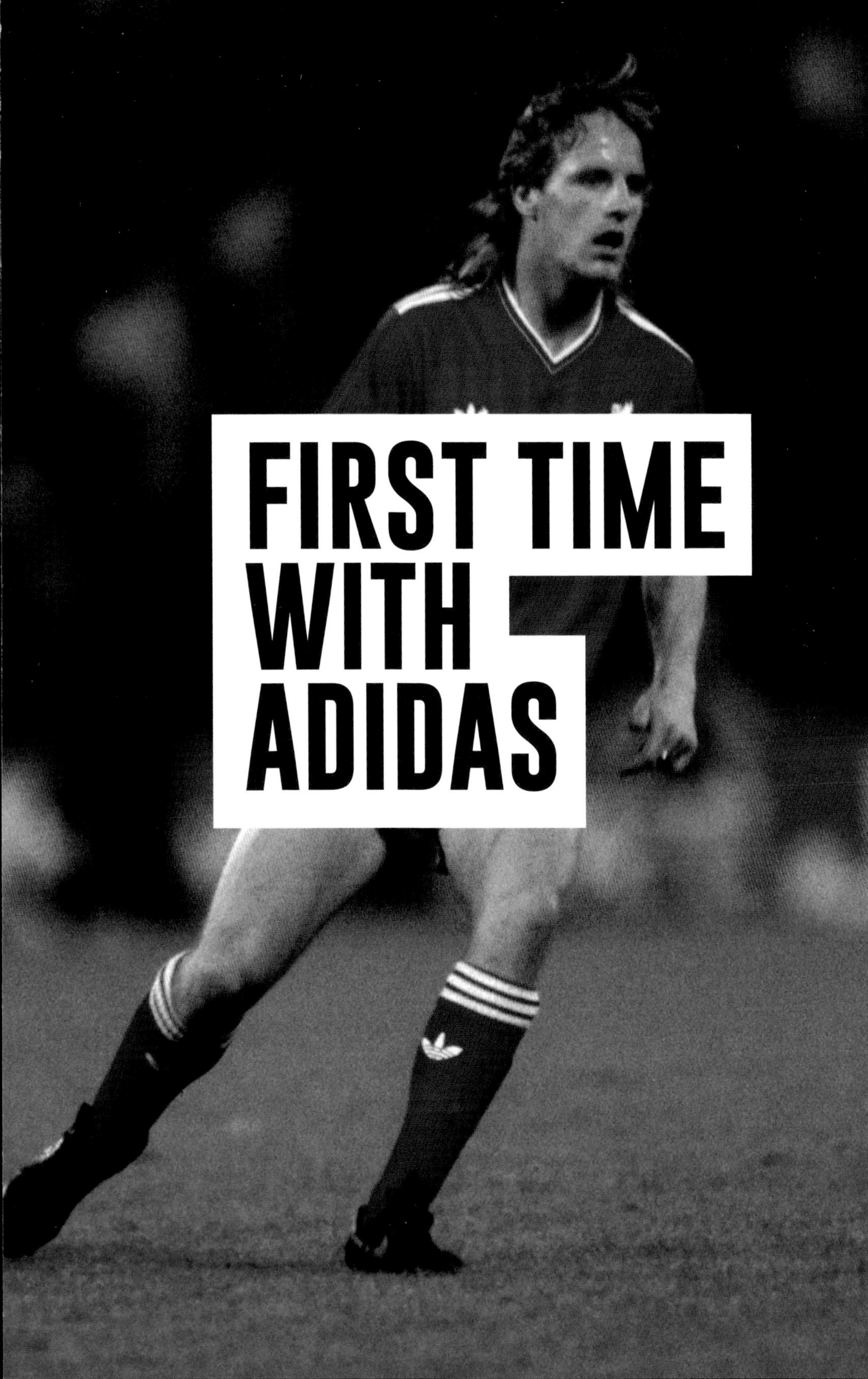

A simple but striking all red Adidas kit featured the manufacturer's trademark three stripes on the shoulders, as well as on the side of the shorts and the tops of the stockings, all in white. With the club badge in white on the heart and the manufacturer's logo opposite, also in white, the sponsor, Crown paints, took the centre, with the word CROWN emblazoned across the chest in white capitals. Kit makers Adidas included a subtle gold trim around the neckline and cuffs of the sleeves. Not noticeable from the stands but visible close-up, the shirt also contained a shadow pattern featuring Liver birds and Adidas stripes.

Kenny Dalglish enjoyed an incredible season in his first as player/manager. Taking to management like a duck to water, he guided Liverpool to a league and FA Cup double. Liverpool became only the fifth club to ever achieve this feat and the first from the north since Preston North End in the Football League's inaugural season of 1888-89.

34 at the start of the campaign, Dalglish restricted himself to playing in exactly half of the league programme and 31 times in all, but he was still invaluable to the side on the pitch. Indeed it was his goal that secured the League Title with a 1-0 victory over Chelsea at Stamford Bridge on the final day of the season. King Kenny also picked himself for the FA Cup final in which a half-time deficit was overturned as the Toffees were well beaten 3-1.

Liverpool's domination of football in this era was based on continuity at the top. From when Bill Shankly took control in 1959 until Dalglish departed from his first stint as gaffer in 1991, the Reds only had four managers – from Shankly to Dalglish, there were four managerial appointments, all appointed from within the club. With Bob Paisley as his assistant, Dalglish had the understanding that, 'If it's working, don't fix it' and so he did not look to make massive changes to a smooth running machine – although since the treble (European Cup, League Title and League Cup) winning season of 1983-84 the Anfield cleaners hadn't required silver polish.

Dalglish did, however, move on ageing full backs who had been as vital to the team as Trent Alexander-Arnold and Andy Robertson are in contemporary times. Having been passed over as Liverpool's new manager, Phil Neal went to Bolton as player/manager on a free in December, while Alan Kennedy joined his home-town club Sunderland for £100,000, followed by goalkeeper Bob Bolder on a free. Incoming were Steve McMahon from Aston Villa for £350,000, Mike Hooper was brought in as a back-up goalkeeper from Wrexham for a £40,000 fee and forward John Durnin was spotted playing for Waterloo Dock, who was receiving £500 for his services. Durnin would only play cup games for Liverpool but went on to have a long and fruitful career elsewhere.

With English clubs banned from Europe, following the tragedy at Heysel where Liverpool lost the European Cup final to Juventus at the end of the season before King Kenny became manager, there was an extra domestic competition called the Screen Sport Super Cup. Liverpool also won this, beating Everton home and away in a two-legged final that was held over to the start of the following season.

WINNERS

There was no European football due to a ban on English clubs.

WINNERS

3-1 win against rivals Everton.

SEMI-FINALS

Eliminated by QPR over two legs.

WINNERS

3-1 win over Norwich City.

42 Goalkeeper Bruce Grobbelaar played all 42 league games and 63 in all.

A group of Liverpool fans headed by Rogan Taylor founded the Football Supporters' Association.

20 Six players reached double figures in the goals column in all competitions with Ian Rush scoring over 30 and Jan Mølby topping 20.

60 Craig Johnston and Alan Hansen each missed just one league game and topped 60 appearances in total.

Total games: 63
Games won: 41
Games drawn: 15
Games lost: 7

KENNY DALGLISH

IAN RUSH

AVERAGE HOME LEAGUE ATTENDANCE 35,271

HIGHEST ATTENDANCE
45,335 VS EVERTON

LOWEST ATTENDANCE
26,219 VS QPR

1988-89 HOME

The season of 1988-89 saw a new sponsor name on the players' shirts. Having been displayed on their shirts since 1982, Crown paints had benefited from massive exposure as part of Liverpool's success story, but now Candy took over.

NEW
SPONSOR
CANDY

Candy made domestic appliances such as dishwashers and washing machines. Based in Milan they were a subsidiary of a Chinese company and before sponsoring Liverpool had invested in Formula One sponsorship. Candy would remain as shirt sponsors until 1992. However, other than the name of the sponsor if you wore a kit from the previous year you were still up to date in terms of the strip itself. Still produced by Adidas, the iconic Liverpool outfit remained blissfully simple and instantly recognisable. Boldly all red with the usual trimmings of three Adidas stripes on the sleeves, the side of the shorts and the tops of the stockings, other than the new sponsor name it was again simply a case of the club badge and manufacturer's logo on the shirt and shorts with the Adidas logo also displayed on the shins of the stockings. As in the previous season the shirt featured a round neck rather than the V-neck seen earlier in the decade.

Having lost sensationally to Wimbledon in the FA Cup final the previous season, a brace from John Aldridge saw Liverpool come from behind to beat the Wombles in the Charity Shield. It was the first of two Wembley wins as a 3-2 FA Cup final win over Everton saw Ian Rush's extra-time brace add to Aldo's opener.

Liverpool came within a minute of also winning the League Title. On a night that spawned the novel and film 'Fever Pitch', Liverpool faced Arsenal at Anfield in the final league game of the season. Going into that game, Liverpool were three points ahead of the Gunners with a goal difference four goals better than their visitors. Liverpool could lose by a goal and still be champions but a two-goal defeat would hand the title to the Londoners by virtue of more goals scored as the teams would be level on points and goal difference.

41,718 were at Anfield while over 12 million watched on television. A cagey game, with Arsenal using David O'Leary as a sweeper, got to half-time goalless. So far so good but Alan Smith nudged Arsenal ahead eight minutes into the second half and the title teetered on the thinnest of knife edges. As referee David Hutchinson's watch ticked beyond 90 minutes it was still 0-1 and the title was still within Liverpool's sights, only for future Liverpool man Michael Thomas to score one of the most dramatic goals in league history with an injury-time goal that made it 0-2 and wrenched the title from Liverpool.

To their immense credit the Kop responded with a rendition of 'We won the cup' – the cup final having taken place six days earlier. More importantly, despite the huge disappointment of seeing a season's work undone in the last moment, ultimately it was a sporting disappointment and everyone present was alive to enjoy the ups and downs of the game. With tragedies like the Hillsborough disaster at the FA Cup semi-final and the horror of Heysel, losing a match paled into insignificance.

RUNNERS-UP

There was still no European football due to a ban on English clubs.

WINNERS

Beating Everton 3-2 in the final.

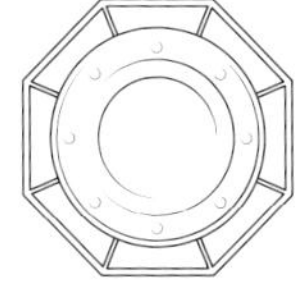

4TH ROUND

Liverpool lost 4-1 to West Ham.

WINNERS

An Aldridge double secures a win against Wimbledon.

52 Steve Nichol and Ray Houghton played all 38 league games and 52 in all.

Liverpool beat Nottingham Forest but lost to Arsenal in the Mercantile Credit League Centenary Trophy.

51 Peter Beardsley and Ronnie Whelan each missed just one league game and made 51 appearances in total.

£2.8M Ian Rush returned to Liverpool at the start of the season in a £2.8m transfer from Juventus – a British record.

31 Behind top scorer Aldridge (31), three other players reached double figures: John Barnes, Peter Beardsley and Ian Rush scoring 14, 12 and 11 goals in all competitions.

KENNY DALGLISH

JOHN ALDRIDGE

AVERAGE HOME LEAGUE ATTENDANCE 38,713

HIGHEST ATTENDANCE 42,518

VS DERBY COUNTY

LOWEST ATTENDANCE 30,283

VS CHARLTON ATHLETIC

1991-92 HOME

Adidas had been producing Liverpool kits since 1985 and, until 1991-92, had satisfied themselves with a relatively modest triple stripe on the shoulders and sleeves of the shirt as well as the shorts, the triple stripe of course being well known to display their branding.

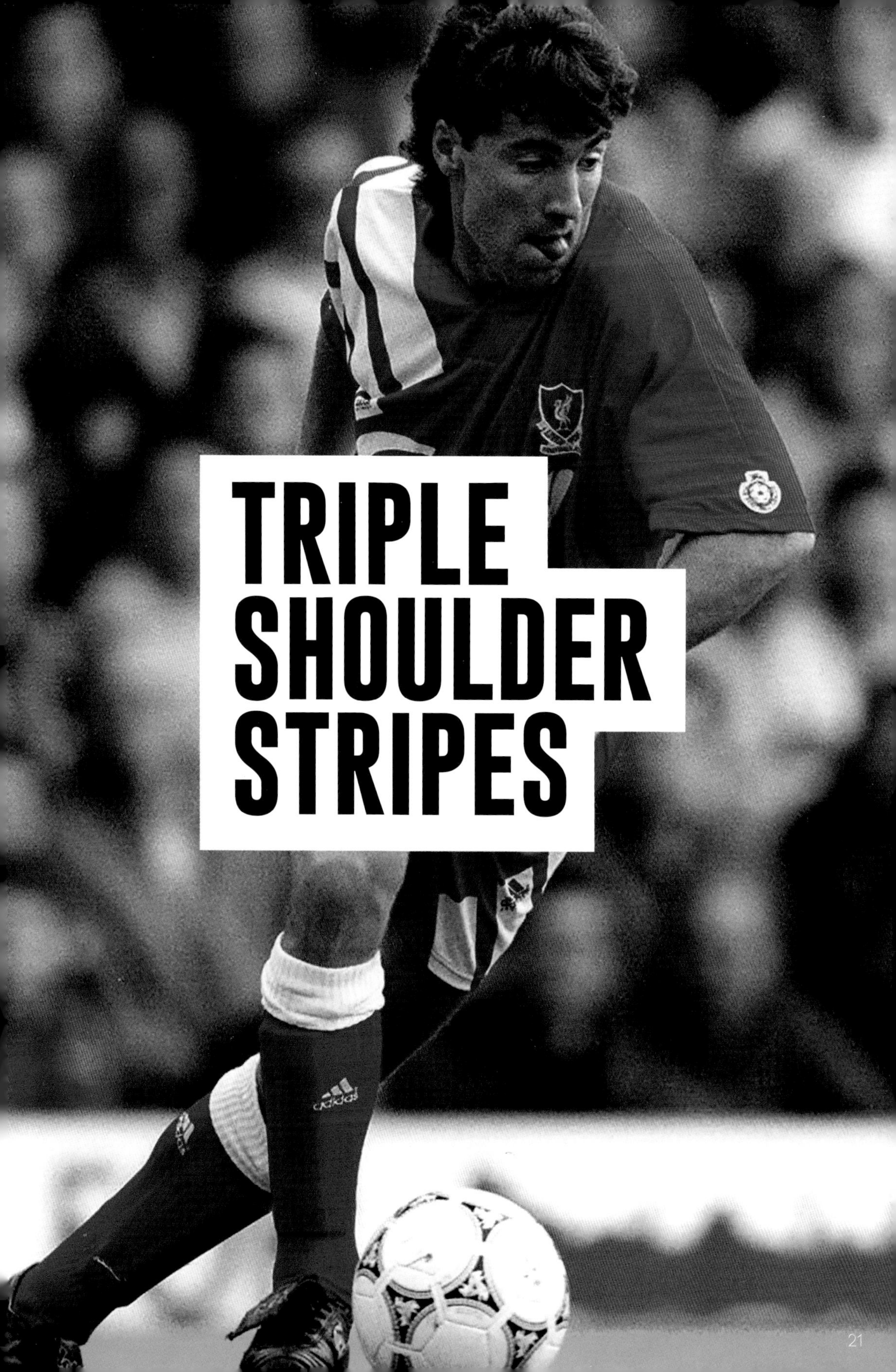

TRIPLE SHOULDER STRIPES

For 1991-92 the manufacturer's branding made a giant leap in terms of how prominent it became as on both the right shoulder and left leg of the shirt and shorts a huge triple stripe encasing the Adidas logo was added. It looked almost as if a huge three-fingered bear had clawed the kit!

To emphasise the large triple white stripes, the rest of the kit was left very simple with the only other embellishments being the club badge in its usual place on the left side of the chest and bottom of the right leg, plus the club sponsor. In white the name of home appliance maker 'Candy' appeared on Liverpool's shirts for the last time. Completing the uniform were white-topped red socks free of the huge Adidas white stripes the other two parts of the kit displayed. Instead a simple name and logo of the company appeared on the shin as it had the season before, although in the spirit of newness and exclusivity the tops had dropped the red hoops of the previous season.

Winning the FA Cup went some way to redeeming a league campaign that was no way to mark the club's 100th season. Pre-season had gone okay with three draws followed by three narrow wins, but there was a sign that all was not well when the dress rehearsal was lost at Tranmere five days before the big kick-off - old boy John Aldridge smacking home Rovers' winner. When the curtain came up on what was the final season before the start of the Premier League, Liverpool fell behind at Anfield to an early goal but edged past Oldham Athletic thanks to John Barnes' 78th-minute winner. It would be one of 13 home wins, but only a late March 4-0 beating of Notts County would see Liverpool score more than three times or win by more than two goals all season in the league.

The problems were away from home where only 13 goals were scored in 21 league games, 11 of which were drawn and only three won, none of them by more than a single goal. While Liverpool were defensively tight on the road – only second-placed Manchester United conceded fewer than Liverpool's 23 away goals – the days of Liverpool outplaying opponents on their own grounds were over, at least for the time being. Much of the autumn was spent in mid-table and although the turn of the year brought the best run of the campaign with four successive league victories that pushed the side up to third, a sequence of just two points from four games followed by an inability to win back-to-back league games for the rest of the season left Liverpool well off the pace. In the final analysis the sixth-placed Reds were six points behind Manchester City in fifth position and 18 adrift of champions Leeds United.

The UEFA Cup did at least bring more goals, 14 being scored in four home games. Just one of those came in the Anfield quarter-final with Genoa who won 2-1 on the night and 4-1 on aggregate, having inflicted Liverpool's third defeat in four foreign trips.

Domestically, in the League Cup, after ending Potteries hopes by knocking out both Stoke City and Port Vale (after a replay), Liverpool came unstuck at Peterborough where they lost 1-0. Replays were required to dispose of Bristol Rovers, Ipswich Town and semi-final opponents Portsmouth (on penalties) in the FA Cup, with Crewe Alexandra and Aston Villa also falling by the wayside. Having won the choice of strips on the toss of a coin, Liverpool wore their home kit in the final as Sunderland were beaten 2-0 - with manager Graeme Souness accompanied by doctors following heart surgery as Ronnie Moran looked after the team.

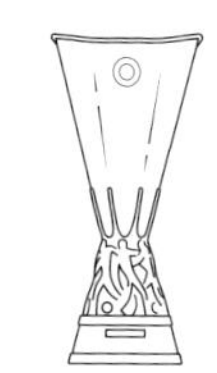

6TH

Liverpool finished outside the top two for the first time since 1981.

WINNERS

The only trophy Graeme Souness won with Liverpool as a manager.

4TH ROUND

Fourth round 1-0 defeat against Peterborough United.

QTR-FINALS

Saunders scored four goals in a 6-2 home win over Kuusysi of Finland.

10 Steve McManaman's 10 assists were almost twice as many as anyone else – five players contributed six each.

41 Just six fewer cup goals were scored compared to league goals: 41 to 47.

Liverpool's centenary season began with a home win against Oldham Athletic.

10 Ten goals from record signing Dean Saunders made him the only player to reach double figures in league goals.

GRAEME SOUNESS

DEAN SAUNDERS

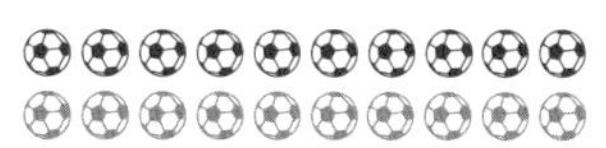

AVERAGE HOME LEAGUE ATTENDANCE
34,799

HIGHEST ATTENDANCE
39,072
VS EVERTON

LOWEST ATTENDANCE
25,457
VS NOTTS COUNTY

1999-2000 HOME

By now in the fourth year of a decade long kit deal with Reebok, this home strip was in the second season of its two-year lifespan. A round collar replaced the V-neck of the previous season's kit.

SIMPLE RED AND ROUND COLLAR

The beauty of the design was in its simplicity which allowed the bold all-red of Liverpool to speak for itself. There was just a thin white stripe on the side of the shorts and a white hoop on the top of the stockings. Manufacturers Reebok had their logo at the bottom of the left leg of the shorts and the right breast of the shirt. The club badge could be found over the heart and the bottom of the right leg of the shorts. Sponsors Carlsberg had their name picked out in white on the chest, with the only other adornment being Premier League patches high up on the sleeves.

Skippered by Jamie Redknapp with Robbie Fowler as his vice-captain, Gérard Houllier's Reds improved on the previous season's seventh place in this season. But while Champions League qualification was welcome, it was a ninth season without a top-two finish, never mind a League Title. The only cup excitement for fans was a 9-2 aggregate win over Hull City in the second round of the League Cup. Defeat in the next round at Southampton quickly squashed hopes of a run in that competition, while in the FA Cup, after a 2-0 win at Huddersfield, Anfield witnessed a disappointing 1-0 home defeat to Blackburn Rovers.

The Premier League season also brought a 1-0 loss (to Watford) in the first home fixture. That was one of two defeats in the first three games and when Everton subsequently won at Anfield on a Monday night at the end of September, it left Liverpool in the bottom half of the table as half of the first eight games had been lost. Improvement came with just one more defeat before Christmas, seeing Liverpool climb to fifth behind Leeds United, Manchester United, Sunderland and Arsenal.

By the time the return derby with Everton came around in April, only two games had been lost in almost seven months. Going into what was a goalless draw at Goodison, Liverpool had climbed to second but there was no question of taking the title as there was an eleven point gap to leaders Manchester United with just five games to go. Sadly it was a tame end to the season as the last five matches failed to produce a goal, a couple of goalless draws accompanying a trio of defeats including one at Bradford City on the final day. The late drop-off was worrying but had Liverpool been closer to the leaders, perhaps fewer late season points would have been surrendered.

There had been considerable investment in the squad with Sami Hyypiä, Vladimír Šmicer and Dietmar Hamann amongst the recruits, while just before the old transfer deadline in March, £11m was invested in Emile Heskey from Leicester City. In a season of progress eyes were cast to the coming campaign, with hopes that there would be better to come.

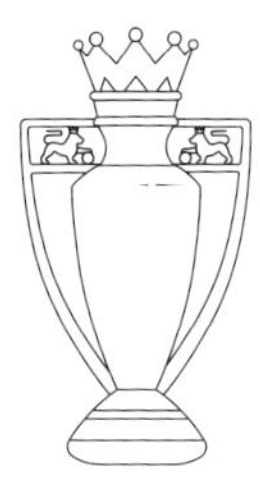

4TH

Liverpool went unbeaten for 13 league games between January and April.

4TH ROUND

Knocked out by Blackburn.

3RD ROUND

A 2-1 loss to Southampton.

42 Sami Hyypiä was ever-present in the league and was the highest appearance maker with 42 games in all.

40 Jamie Carragher was the only other player to reach 40 appearances.

12 Only Michael Owen with 12 and Titi Camara with 10 reached double figures in the goal charts.

Liverpool had the tightest defence in the league in away games, conceding five goals fewer than anyone else.

AVERAGE HOME LEAGUE ATTENDANCE

44,074

HIGHEST ATTENDANCE

44,929

VS MANCHESTER UNITED

LOWEST ATTENDANCE

40,483

VS BRADFORD CITY

2006-07 HOME

After a decade of Reebok-made kits, Adidas returned as Liverpool's supplier. Inevitably the trademark three Adidas stripes made an instant return but the sportswear company satisfied themselves with straightforward, discreet white stripes on the sleeves and sides of the shorts, along with three white hoops at the top of the stockings, which also carried an Adidas logo.

A RETURN TO ADIDAS

The main introduction to the kit was the addition of a thin white outline on the trunk. From a distance it looked almost like the shape of a vase, the thin tapering off at the top leading to the collar. A central Adidas emblem was encased within the outline, as was the Carlsberg sponsor name in white and the club badge in its usual place.

Special match-related embroidery was added for the Champions League final and Community Shield matches, while in some Champions League away matches (such as at Bordeaux) shirts without the Carlsberg sponsorship were worn due to bans on alcohol sponsorship in those areas. The following season in 2007-08 Liverpool basically wore the same shirt with very minor amendments such as the size of the sponsor logo and updated Premier League sleeve badges.

A run to the Champions League final was the highlight of a season in which, off the pitch, Liverpool – a club famed for continuity – underwent significant change. February saw Tom Hicks and George Gillett take over from David Moores as chairman. The Moores family had been invested in Liverpool for more than half a century, in which time Liverpool had risen from the second division to become the country's most successful club. The American duo took over with LFC valued at just under £220m, Liverpool following Manchester United and Aston Villa in coming under American ownership, but Hicks and Gillett proved to be unpopular owners.

On the pitch, four defeats in the first nine games got the campaign off to a bad start, these including four consecutive away losses without scoring. This left Liverpool in the bottom half of the table with only half as many points as front-runners Manchester United and Chelsea. A run of nine wins from 10 games from the start of December then saw a climb to third by the end of January, but the gap to the top had only been reduced by three points. The damage had been done and Liverpool would finish third having fallen away badly. Ahead of Arsenal only narrowly on goal difference, Benítez's boys finished a massive 15 points behind runners-up Chelsea and a monstrous 21 away from winners Manchester United.

Arsenal ended Liverpool's interest early in both domestic cups, but in Europe serene progress was made through the qualifying round and group stage of the Champions League. The knockout stage saw an excellent 2-1 win at Barcelona be just enough to edge through on away goals after a 1-0 Anfield defeat. PSV Eindhoven were then comfortably taken care of before a semi-final tie with José Mourinho's Chelsea, who took a 1-0 lead at Stamford Bridge. Daniel Agger quickly cancelled that out at Anfield but with no further scoring the game went to penalties where Liverpool held their nerve to triumph.

It could have been an all-England final but Manchester United lost to AC Milan who therefore met Liverpool in Athens. Although Dirk Kuyt pulled a goal back after Milan went 2-0 up, there was to be no equaliser as there had been two years earlier at the famous fightback final between the clubs in Istanbul. Other than the Community Shield, Liverpool finished the season trophyless and with new American owners as fans looked to a future with an unusual sense of uncertainty.

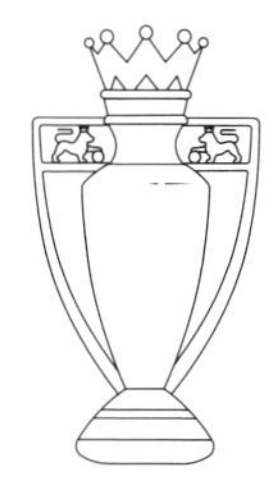

3RD

Biggest home wins being 4-0 against Fulham & Sheff Utd.

3RD ROUND

3-1 home defeat against Arsenal.

QTR -FINALS

Arsenal knocking Liverpool out 6-3.

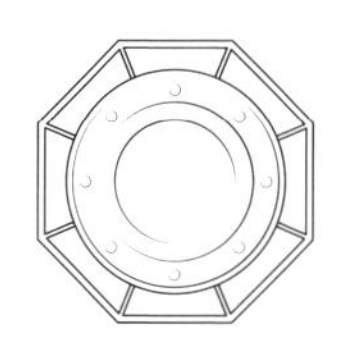

WINNERS

2-1 win against Chelsea at the Millennium Stadium.

RUNNERS-UP

Liverpool took part in their seventh European Cup final.

52 With 52 appearances, Jermaine Pennant played in more games than anyone else.

Jamie Carragher, Steven Gerrard, Xabi Alonso and Pepe Reina all played 51 times.

Dirk Kuyt was the only man to reach double figures of Premier League goals.

33 players made a first team appearance.

1.5% Gates were down by over 1.5% on the previous season.

9 Pennant and Steve Finnan contributed most assists with 9 and 8 respectively.

RAFA BENÍTEZ

PETER CROUCH

AVERAGE HOME LEAGUE ATTENDANCE 43,563

HIGHEST ATTENDANCE
44,403 VS MAN UNITED

LOWEST ATTENDANCE
41,370 VS BOLTON WDR

2011-12 HOME

This was the last season of the club's six-year deal with Adidas, with the same kit as worn in the previous season. From a distance the shirt had a classically traditional look but close-up there was a background pattern that looked something like bunting – perhaps anticipating the winning of a trophy.

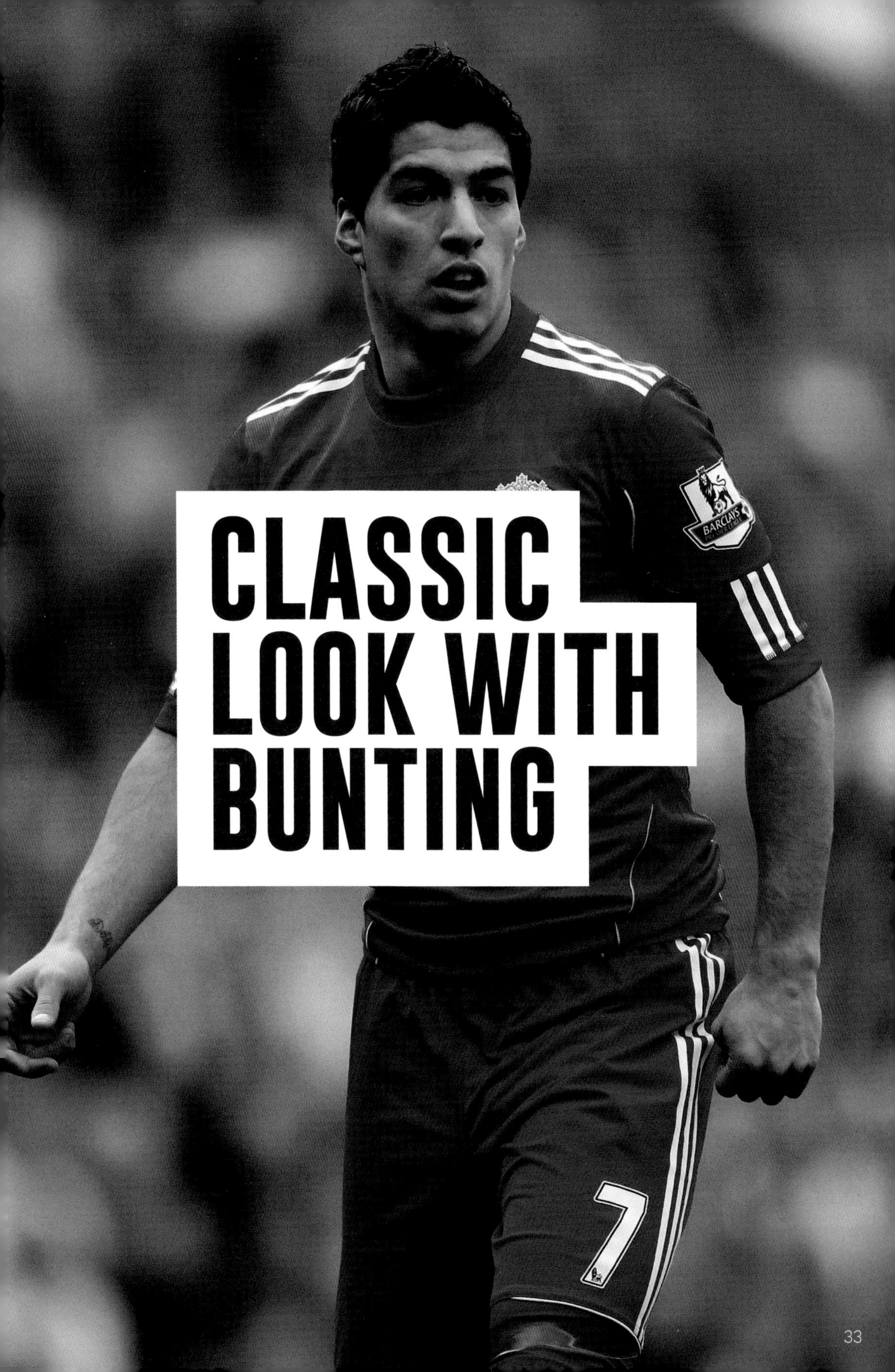
CLASSIC
LOOK WITH
BUNTING

The Adidas branding was much less obvious than in some previous Liverpool kits. Even the standard three stripes on the sleeve were not so prominent as a break in the stripes high on the sleeve allowed the Premier League badges to be seen unhindered. With a round collar the shirt included the manufacturer's logo and club badge, as was normal, with the name and logo of sponsors Standard Chartered in white. The player's name and number were also in white on the back of the shirt. Similarly the shorts and socks had a simple appeal. The club badge on the shorts and Adidas logo on the socks were the only additions to the basic red, other than the obligatory three white Adidas stripes on the side of the shorts and three white hoops on the stocking tops.

For the first time since the 1999-2000 season, European football was absent from Anfield. Under Kenny Dalglish both domestic cup finals were reached, one of which was won on penalties, but it was an enormously disappointing season in the Premier League. They finished eighth – the club's joint-lowest position since being promoted in 1962 – and even then only just edged ahead of ninth-placed Fulham on goal difference. Despite winning the League Cup and reaching the FA Cup final, manager and club legend Kenny Dalglish was sacked at the end of the season.

He had been backed in the transfer market: £20m was spent on Stewart Downing, £16m on a young Jordan Henderson and £5m-£7m each on Sebastian Coates, Charlie Adam and Jose Enrique - and all this after upwards of £30m had been spent on Andy Carroll in the previous transfer window.

Taking seven points from the first nine was a good start but when a 1-0 loss at Stoke was followed by a 4-0 defeat at Tottenham, it sent out early warning signs that the campaign had the potential to be a difficult one. Nonetheless, with just one more league loss in the remainder of the calendar year, 2011 ended with the Reds fifth in the table - but with a monumental 11-point gap to leaders Manchester City who had played one less game. At this stage Liverpool were unbeaten at home but over half those home games had been drawn. They were struggling for goals having scored only half as many on their own patch as the two Manchester clubs had, despite having played more games on their own ground.

2012 then started badly in the Premier League with only one point from the first three games with worse soon to follow, as the team suffered six defeats in the next seven games– the crumb of comfort being a 3-0 win over Everton in the middle of that run. Subsequently things went from bad to worse with 11 of the last 19 Premier League games lost.

Such dismal league form was disguised by cup results. Manchester City were beaten over two legs in the League Cup semi-final. Liverpool were hot favourites to win the final against Cardiff City but hard work was made of it, before a penalty shoot-out win for the Bluebirds – despite Steven Gerrard and Charlie Adam failing with the first two penalties. Goal-shy at home for much of the season, Liverpool were drawn at home in every round of the FA Cup, scoring 15 goals in the process with Manchester United amongst the victims. Everton were then beaten in the semi-final but in the final they fell two goals behind to Chelsea. Andy Carroll managed to reduce the deficit mid-way through the second half but they just couldn't draw level (afterwards).

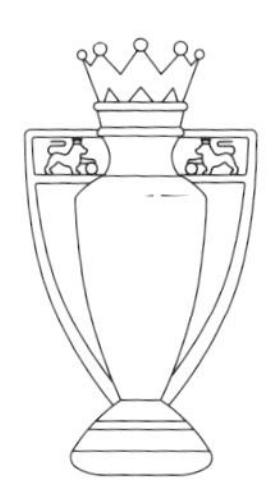

8TH

This was Liverpool's 50th successive season in the top flight.

RUNNERS-UP

Beaten by Chelsea 2-1.

WINNERS

Liverpool beat Cardiff 2-3 on penalties.

11 11 of the last 19 Premier League games were lost.

17 Luis Suárez was the only player to reach double figures in the goal stakes, in all competitions.

6 Six goals were enough to make Craig Bellamy the club's second-highest Premier League scorer.

48 In his first season Jordan Henderson played 48 games, across all competitions.

AVERAGE HOME LEAGUE ATTENDANCE

44,253

HIGHEST ATTENDANCE

45,065 VS MANCHESTER UNITED

LOWEST ATTENDANCE

40,106 VS FULHAM

KENNY DALGLISH

LUIS SUÁREZ

2017-18 HOME

To commemorate 125 years of Liverpool FC, New Balance came up with a kit to keep traditionalists happy. A straightforward, bold red shirt with a white collar and sleeve edges was accompanied by the sponsor Standard Chartered's name in white along with the manufacturer's logo.

125 YEAR COMMEMORATIVE KIT

A very smart and simple club badge showed a gold liver bird above the letters L.F.C. and the words, '125 years'. Either side of the liver bird the dates 1892-2017 showed the timespan of the club. The same club badge and wording appeared on the right leg of the all-red shorts, with the New Balance logo on the left leg and the socks having L.F.C. in gold on the shins of white-topped red socks. Significantly, another number appeared on the back of the shirts alongside the '125' and the individual player's number: just under the collar in gold lettering the number 96 appeared as part of the logo. This of course was a nod to the Justice for the 96 campaign, who fought for recognition of those who tragically lost their lives at the Hillsborough disaster. A 97th victim of that horrific event was subsequently recognised in 2021 when Andrew Stanley Devine passed away as a result of the life-changing injuries he suffered in the disaster.

This season was all about the Champions League and the highs and lows of football. In the Premier League, Liverpool never topped the table; a couple of weeks in second spot in the spring being the best they could do before eventually finishing fourth, 25 points behind champions Manchester City. The Reds were the only team to have an unbeaten home record in the Premier League, but only 15th-placed Brighton and wooden spooners West Brom drew more at home. Bottom club West Brom did however win at Anfield in the FA Cup, with Liverpool's League Cup campaign falling at the first hurdle at Leicester.

Mo Salah took everyone/everywhere by storm. The Egyptian forward scored on his debut and ended up with more than double the number of Premier League goals than second-top marksman Roberto Firmino, duly taking the Player and Players' Player of the Season accolades as a result.

In the Champions League Liverpool were incredible. They came through the qualifying round and group stage unbeaten, beating two of their three group opponents 7-0. They then won 5-0 away to Porto in the round of 16 before finishing the job at home. The quarter-finals were even better. Manchester City may have run away with the Premier League Title but when faced with European royalty they had to bow down. Beaten 3-0 at Anfield, City hopes of a Blue Moon were raised when Gabriel Jesus scored in only the second minute of the return leg, only for Liverpool to go on and win on the night with two second-half goals. Pep Guardiola missed a close-up view having been ejected from the technical area at half time!

The result took Liverpool to Kyiv in Ukraine for the final against defending champions Real Madrid. There were tears from Salah as the goal machine had to go off injured in the first half, but he was not the Liverpool player to be most upset afterwards. Goalkeeper Loris Karius dropped two of the biggest howlers in the history of the final as Liverpool lost 3-1, one of the keeper's mistakes giving Gareth Bale his second goal of the night after the Welshman had already scored with a superb bicycle kick. If ever a Liverpool player was left to walk alone it was Karius, who seemed to endure an almost total lack of consolatory hugs or handshakes from distraught teammates as he tearfully tried to apologise to fans. Afterwards Merseyside Police reportedly investigated death threats towards the goalkeeper who was later revealed to have suffered from concussion in the game before his costly errors. Subsequently loaned out, by March 2022 Karius remained a Liverpool player but had never played a competitive game for the club since his disastrous night in Kyiv.

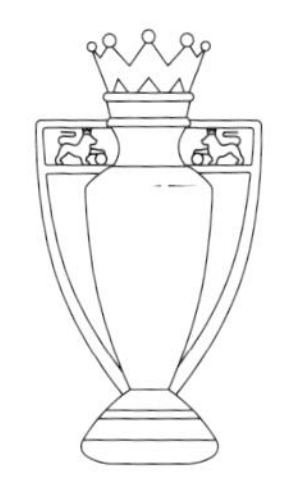

4TH

Biggest defeat being 5-0 against Man City.

4TH ROUND

3-2 defeat to West Brom.

3RD ROUND

2-0 defeat to Leicester City.

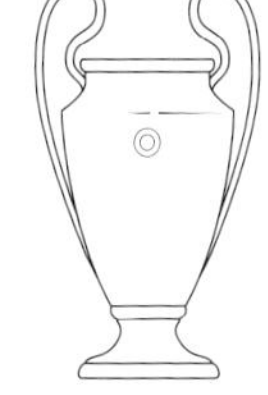

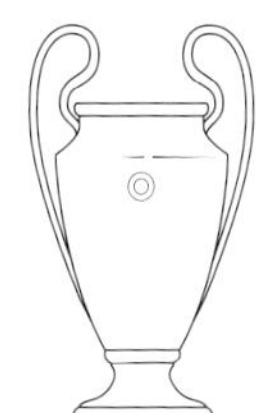

RUNNERS-UP

Liverpool took part in their eighth European Cup final.

2-1 Leicester were beaten 2-1 in Hong Kong in the pre-season Premier League Asia Trophy final.

7-0 A 7-0 Champions League away win at Maribor equalled the record away win in the competition.

£36.5M A club-record £36.5m rising to £43m was well spent on Mo Salah.

£8M £8m spent on Scottish left-back Andy Robertson.

Firmino, Salah and Mané all reached double figures in the scoring charts – just in Champions League goals.

After beating Bayern Munich, the pre-season Audi Cup final was lost on penalties to Atlético Madrid in Munich.

JÜRGEN KLOPP

MO SALAH

AVERAGE HOME LEAGUE ATTENDANCE 53,059

HIGHEST ATTENDANCE 53,287

VS NEWCASTLE AND WATFORD

LOWEST ATTENDANCE 50,752

VS BRIGHTON & HOVE ALBION

AY

1986-87 AWAY

Having moved from an all-yellow to an all-white away kit in 1985-86 when Adidas took over from Umbro, in the second season of the Adidas contract, the white away kit remained but with the introduction of black shorts. As in the previous season an all-yellow strip was retained as a third choice kit.

SIMPLE WHITE VARIANT

Keeping with the tradition of Liverpool shirts, both home and away, the top was nice and simple, making teammate identification on the pitch that split-second quicker than with more complicated designs. Featuring a red V-neck and cuffs, the top was all white with the exception of the crown paints (Crown now in all lower case rather than capitals as per the season before) sponsor name in red, along with the club badge and the distinctive triple Adidas stripe on the shoulders. On the back the numbers were also in red.

Having been double winners in Dalglish's first season as player/manager, in King Kenny's second year the only trophies Liverpool saw were a share in the Charity Shield after a Wembley draw with Everton and the Screen Sport Super Cup – this being a short-lived competition where the previous season's final (also against Everton) had been held over to the start of this one! There was also a penalty shoot-out December victory over Celtic in the Dubai Super Cup but really this was no more than a mid-season sunshine break and a glorified friendly.

Ian Rush scored a fabulous 40 goals in his final season in red before heading to Italy where he signed for Juventus. One of his strikes put Liverpool – wearing the white away kit – into the lead in the League Cup final against Arsenal, only for the Gunners to come back and win with a brace from Charlie Nicholas.

Defeats were too common in the league for a team seeking to be champions – over a quarter of league games were lost. A 12-match unbeaten run starting two days after Christmas was the only long unbeaten sequence in the season but when this was followed by five losses in seven games it illustrated that Liverpool were off the pace, finishing nine points behind champions and local rivals Everton. And yet in the middle of this bad run Everton were defeated 3-1 at Anfield. As Liverpool well know, it is consistency that wins leagues and in this season the Reds didn't have enough of it.

The FA Cup also brought disappointment as Liverpool lost out to Luton at the first hurdle, when the Reds failed to score in a three-game tie. In contrast there were goals galore in the League Cup starting with a 10-0 hammering of Fulham where Steve McMahon got a hat-trick. Everton were beaten at Goodison in the quarter-final, before ultimately the final was lost to the Gunners.

RUNNERS-UP

There was no European football due to a ban on English clubs.

3RD ROUND

It took two replays for Luton to eliminate Liverpool.

RUNNERS-UP

Rush scores but Liverpool lose out 2-1 against Arsenal.

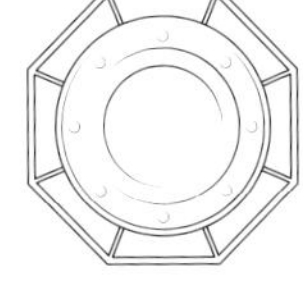

JOINT WINNERS

Shared with Everton.

14 Ian Rush was a one-man goal rush! Second-top scorer Steve McMahon netted 14 - 26 fewer than Rush.

Barry Venison, Steve Staunton, John Aldridge and Nigel Spackman were amongst the new signings.

10-0 The lowest attendance of the season witnessed the biggest win – 10-0 v Fulham.

57 Five players played 50 or more games, Ian Rush topping the list with 57.

Sammy Lee left to move to QPR.

25 25th consecutive year in the top-flight.

KENNY DALGLISH

IAN RUSH

AVERAGE HOME LEAGUE ATTENDANCE

36,284

HIGHEST ATTENDANCE

44,827

VS EVERTON

LOWEST ATTENDANCE

13,498

VS FULHAM (LEAGUE CUP)

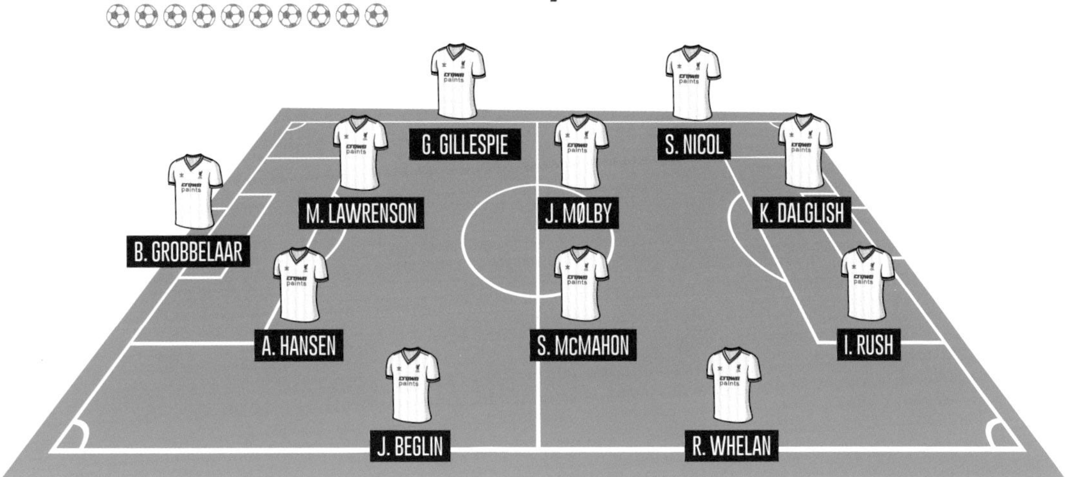

1990-91 AWAY

In a change from their traditional red kit, Liverpool sported an all-grey kit trimmed in red. Grey had been instituted in previous seasons kits with the 1990-91 change kit being worn for a second season having been introduced in the 1987-89 season.

GREY SHADED DIAMONDS

Unlike the 1987-89 shirt which was a simple grey, this one consisted of a white base with grey shaded diamonds in a diagonal pattern, giving it a very modern but sportingly indistinct appearance. The risqué novel 'Fifty Shades of Grey' wasn't published for another decade but perhaps this kit contributed to inspiring it!

The usual trimmings were in evidence: the club badge, sponsor name (Candy) and Adidas logo all in their usual places in red, as were the three Adidas stripes on the sleeves which had red cuffs. The neckline was also picked out in red. Shorts and socks were all grey – rather than grey on a white base like the shirt. The red stripes on the shorts and hoops on the stocking tops were brighter than on the 1987-89 away kit but the manufacturer's logo on the socks remained in the same place on the shin, as did the club badge and Adidas logo on the shorts - with the Liverpool emblem on the right leg and the Adidas one on the left.

With Liverpool top of the table in late February, manager Kenny Dalglish rocked Anfield by suddenly resigning, stating 'personal reasons' for his decision. The team were in the thick of the season's action when King Kenny's bombshell landed, just 24 hours before a shell-shocked team lost 3-1 at Luton Town. Arsenal's 4-0 victory over Crystal Palace the same day took them just above Liverpool, with the Gunners due to come to Anfield the following weekend. In that game, a goal from Paul Merson had the away fans performing an unwanted rendition of '1-0 to the Arsenal' as Liverpool's unbeaten record was ended. A bad week was made even worse when, having drawn 4-4 at Goodison Park in Dalglish's last game, in an FA Cup replay, in between the Luton and Arsenal games a second replay with Everton was lost 1-0. Ronnie Moran took charge of the team from Dalglish's departure; winning four, drawing one and losing five games in the league and cup before Graeme Souness was installed as the new boss. Moran's wins included a 7-1 win over Derby and a 5-4 victory against Leeds. Life certainly wasn't dull! Souness ended the campaign with three wins and two defeats, but in another season without European football and with early exits in both domestic cups, falling one place short in the title race was disappointing – especially as champions Arsenal had two points deducted for their part in a brawl with Manchester United. Liverpool had lost the title. What nobody knew at the time or could contemplate is that they would not regain it for 30 years.

RUNNERS-UP

A record was set when Liverpool finished in the top two for a 10th successive season.

5TH ROUND

Everton beat Liverpool after two replays.

3RD ROUND

A 3-1 loss to Manchester United.

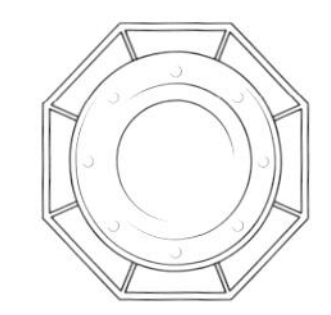

JOINT WINNERS

Shared with Manchester United.

40 Six players played 40 or more games, Ian Rush topping the list with 48.

16 John Barnes was joint-top league scorer with 16 goals along with Ian Rush, who had 26 goals in all competitions.

Liverpool were still banned from Europe following the terrible Heysel disaster.

Skipper Alan Hansen announced his retirement.

AVERAGE HOME LEAGUE ATTENDANCE **36,038**

HIGHEST ATTENDANCE **38,463** VS CHELSEA

LOWEST ATTENDANCE **31,063** VS COVENTRY CITY

KENNY DALGLISH Until 22nd Feb

RONNIE MORAN 22nd Feb to 16th April

GRAEME SOUNESS from 16th April

IAN RUSH

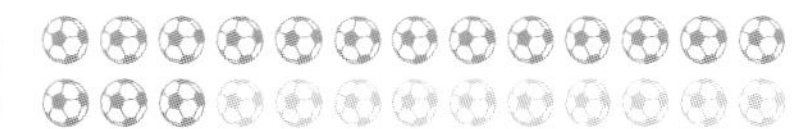

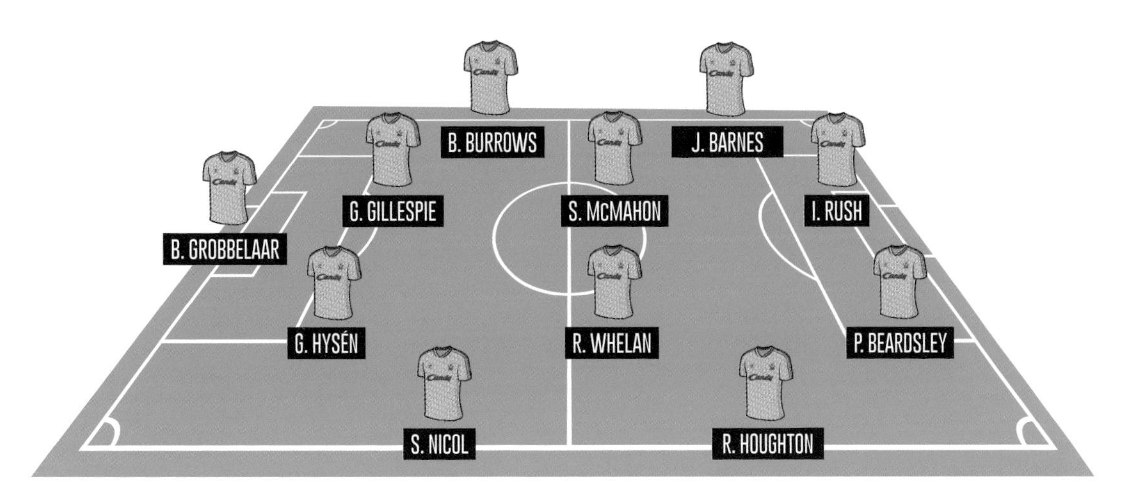

1991-92 AWAY

Produced by Adidas the shirt was a bold green affair with green even used for the words 'Liverpool Football Club' on the green and white club badge. Three very broad white stripes on the right shoulder represented the trademark of the manufacturers Adidas.

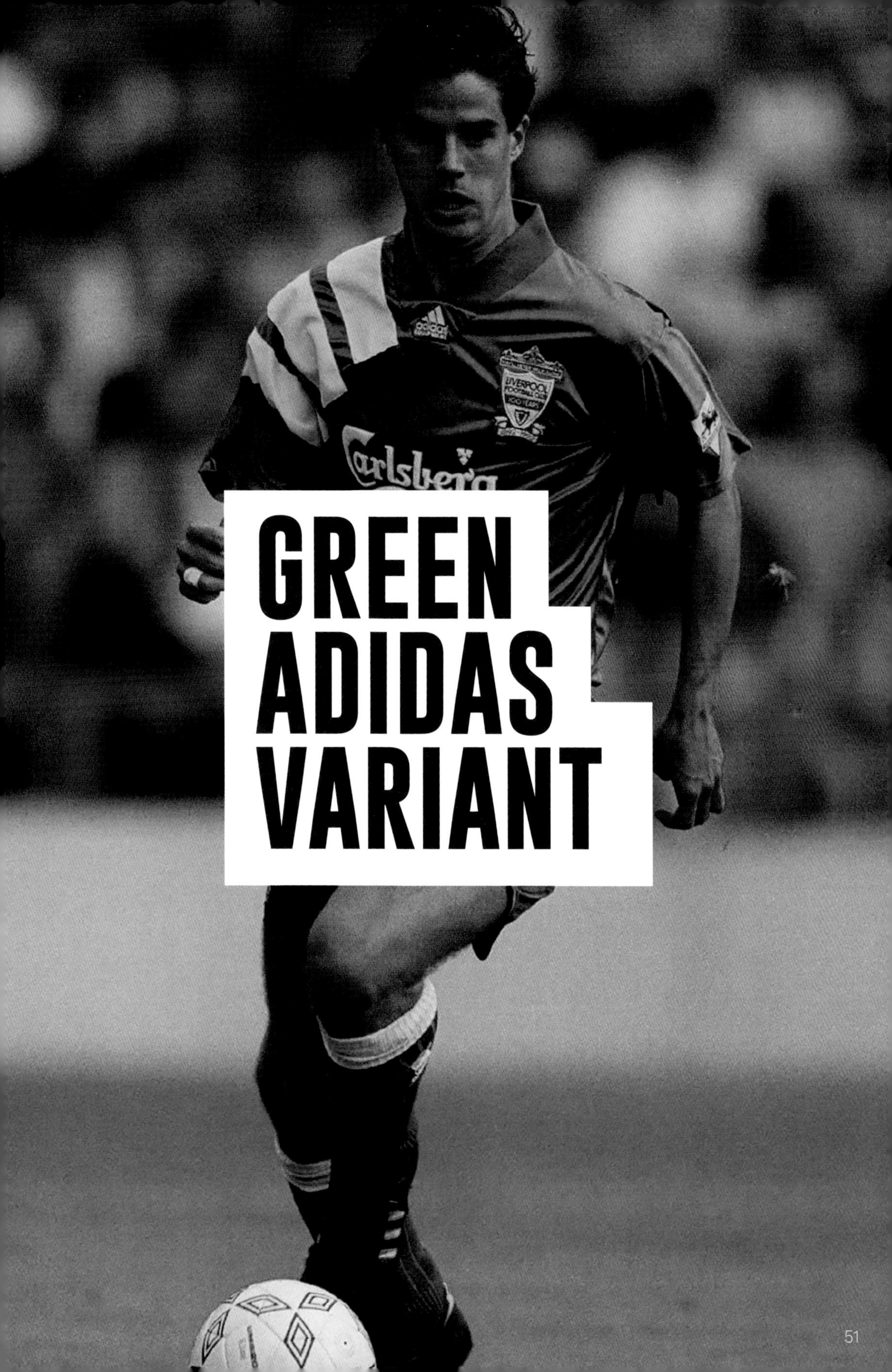

GREEN ADIDAS VARIANT

The bottom of the middle of these stripes bore the Adidas name and logo in green with the shirt sponsor Candy's name in white. With a very slightly different shade of green on the sleeve edges and V-necked collar, the shirt was a modern and attractive top other than for those traditionalists who only like to see goalkeepers in green. Green was a totally new colour for Liverpool outfield players, although since its introduction it has often been used for Liverpool kits, not only by Adidas but also Reebok and New Balance.

The shoulder stripes carried over onto the reverse of the shirt which, in keeping with the front, also used white for the player number. In what was the last year of Liverpool's membership of the Football League before the start of the Premier League, small Football League badges appeared on the sleeves.

The shirt was usually paired with white shorts featuring the trio of bold self-promoting Adidas stripes in green on the left leg, but sometimes green shorts were used. Regardless of whether white or green shorts were worn, green socks with white tops completed the kit.

Liverpool's 100th season was commemorated by the winning of the FA Cup, but it was far from a vintage campaign otherwise. The previous ten years had seen a dominant Liverpool finish in the top two every season, being champions on six of those occasions. In fact the 1991-92 season was only the second time in 20 years that Liverpool had not finished in the top two and was the club's lowest finish since 1965 when they won the FA Cup for the first time.

The UEFA Cup campaign ended at the quarter-final stage. Defeat at Genoa was a third away loss in four trips in the competition, with the Italians coming to Anfield to win again in what was a disappointing season other than that low key FA Cup campaign. Winning the FA Cup in 1992 was something of a slog rather than a parade of invincibility. Already eliminated from the League Cup at the hands of Peterborough, replays were required to knock out second division sides Bristol Rovers and Ipswich in the fourth and fifth rounds. A 1-0 quarter-final win over Aston Villa overcame the only top-flight opposition encountered in the whole run. In the semi-final, second division Portsmouth were only beaten on penalties after a replay, before the final pitted Liverpool against a Sunderland side who had endured such a poor season in the second tier that they were the lowest ranked finalists since Leicester City in 1949. At Wembley, Republic of Ireland international John Byrne, having scored in every round for the Wearsiders so far, missed a sitter at 0-0, otherwise Liverpool could have struggled. But with Steve McManaman in magnificent form, second half goals from Michael Thomas and Ian Rush delivered a newly made FA Cup for manager Graeme Souness - who was surrounded by doctors to help keep him calm just a month after he had undergone heart surgery.

Thomas' Wembley goal came just a couple of years after his famous, late strike for Arsenal snatched the title from Liverpool. Thomas also created the second goal for Rush who recorded a record fifth Wembley FA Cup final goal. Somewhat awkwardly, at the presentations Liverpool were mistakenly given runners-up medals and had to exchange them with their Sunderland counterparts on the pitch.

88 88 goals were scored in total but just 47 in the league.

55 Six players played 50 or more games, Bruce Grobbelaar topping the list with 55.

10 Ten players including Mark Wright and Jamie Redknapp made their Liverpool debuts.

23 Only runners-up Man United let in fewer than Liverpool's 23 goals conceded on the road.

46 Ray Houghton and Steve McManaman joined top scorer Saunders in reaching double figures.

The trio netted 46 between them in all competitions.

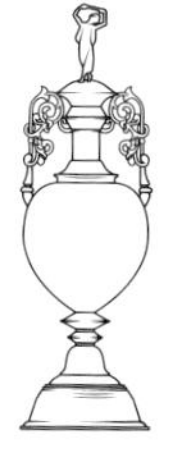

6TH

Liverpool were the lowest away scorers in the league with just 13 goals.

WINNERS

2-0 win over Sunderland.

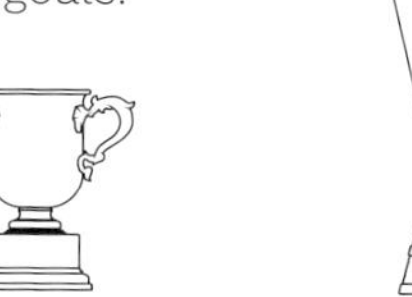

4TH ROUND

1-0 defeat to Peterborough United.

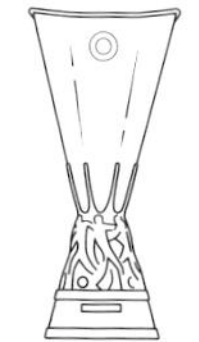

QTR-FINALS

6-0 over two legs against FC Swarovski Tirol in the third round.

 **GRAEME SOUNESS**

 **DEAN SAUNDERS**

AVERAGE HOME LEAGUE ATTENDANCE 34,799

HIGHEST ATTENDANCE 39,072

VS EVERTON

LOWEST ATTENDANCE 25,457

VS NOTTS COUNTY

1995-96 AWAY

Quartered shirts are more the preserve of rugby teams than association football clubs. While Bristol Rovers' blue and white quartered shirts are distinctive, English teams generally play in plain or striped shirts with just a handful having different coloured sleeves to the rest of the top and a smattering preferring hoops. Therefore when Liverpool sported green and white quartered shirts in 1995-96 it was a kit unusual in design if not colour.

GREEN AND WHITE QUARTERS

Green had been the dominant colour of the Anfielders' first choice away kit since 1991 when it was introduced by Adidas, who continued to produce the playing strip - although this was the final year of their contract with the club. Whereas in previous seasons the body of the shirt had been dominantly either green or white with green sleeves, the introduction of quarters represented a new look for Liverpool fans. The back of the shirt was all-white, enabling the numbers to be easily seen. With one white sleeve and one green one, the shirt was even more unusual to ones that had gone before. The club badge was picked out in green on a white background above the heart with the word 'Adidas' in white against a green base on the opposite side. The sponsor name Carlsberg was in black in the centre of the shirt which, being green and white, matched Carlsberg's corporate colours.

For the first time green shorts were introduced, with white socks, the shorts and socks were simple in design. The shorts included the normal triple Adidas stripes down the side, while the socks featured green and white hoops on the tops.

The FA Cup final was reached but this was far from a vintage season. Liverpool were third in the Premier League but there was a gaping 11-point chasm to champions Manchester United. Liverpool also lost to United in the cup final on a day when defences were on top until Eric Cantona snatched the trophy with an 85th minute strike. It was only the second goal Liverpool had conceded in the competition all season.

There was also little joy to be had from the other cup competitions, with early exits in the League and UEFA Cups; Liverpool failing to score in three of their four games in the UEFA Cup, going out tamely at home to Brøndby of Denmark.

In the league, while five of the opening seven games were won there were 1-0 defeats at Leeds and Wimbledon. There was a decent 15-game unbeaten run in the middle of the season and only two defeats after November, following a costly sequence of just a single point from four games, but overall Roy Evans' side were off the pace. Even in mid-March when Liverpool trailed United by just two points with eight games to go, Liverpool were also two points behind second-placed Newcastle, who had two games in hand. In the final analysis both Uniteds pulled away, Liverpool lagging seven points behind the second-placed Magpies.

3RD

League attendances were 15% up on the previous season.

RUNNERS-UP

Manchester United beat Liverpool 1-0 in the final.

4TH ROUND

Knocked out by Newcastle United.

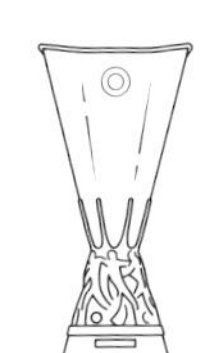

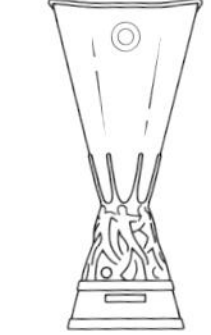

2ND ROUND

Knocked out 1-0 by Brøndby IF.

5 Away from home they were only joint fifth-top scorers with just one more goal scored away than bottom club Bolton.

53 David James, Steve McManaman and Robbie Fowler all played 53 games in all competitions with John Barnes also appearing 50 times.

£8.5M A club record £8.5m was paid for Stan Collymore.

Ian Rush was given a free transfer at the end of the season.

Liverpool scored more Premier League goals at home than anyone else.

£4.5M £4.5m was spent on Jason McAteer from Bolton Wanderers.

ROY EVANS

ROBBIE FOWLER

AVERAGE HOME LEAGUE ATTENDANCE
39,553

HIGHEST ATTENDANCE
40,820
VS CHELSEA

LOWEST ATTENDANCE
34,063
VS COVENTRY CITY

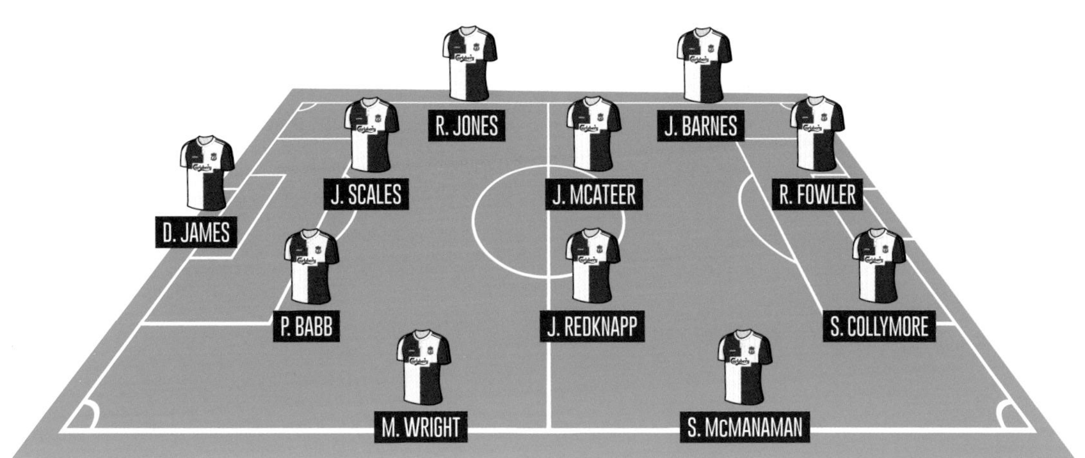

1999-2000 AWAY

"Styled with passion, worn with pride" was the strapline on match programme adverts for the Reebok away kit which re-introduced green as the main colour. Until the early 1990s green had only been seen as part of the goalkeeper's kit, before Adidas brought it in as a radical change in 1991-92.

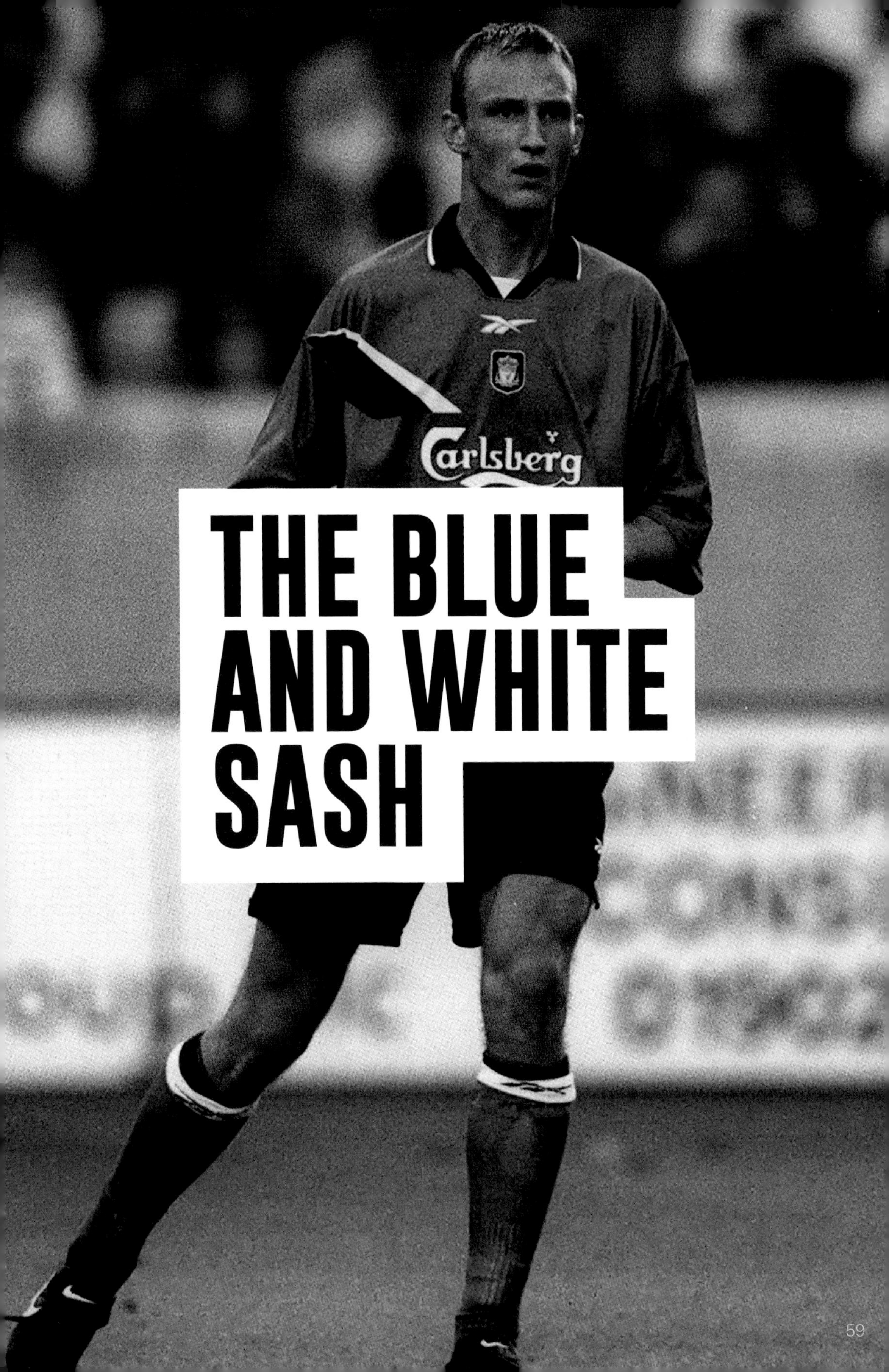

THE BLUE AND WHITE SASH

There was a slight tweak a year later, another kit with a lot of green to follow and then a green and white quartered shirt – in the Bristol Rovers style – before yellow and white away kits preceded the 1999-2000 strip.

Given football is played on grass it always seems strange to choose green for kits in a sport where split-second teammate identification is vital. Having said that, the strip was undoubtedly stylish. A bright green with a dark blue collar that matched the dark blue shorts, the shirt featured a central club badge beneath the manufacturer's logo. Sponsor Carlsberg's name was picked out in white in the centre of a diagonal dark blue and white stripe. White was also seen on the stocking tops that showed the Reebok logo in dark blue on the otherwise green hosiery.

Following Steven Gerrard's breakthrough in 1998-99 (when he featured 13 times), Manager Gérard Houllier selected the young midfielder for the first home game of the 1999-2000 season, against Watford. Houllier then kept him in the side for the following seven matches. Four games into that run Stevie G made his England Under-21 debut, scoring the opening goal in a 5-0 thrashing of Luxembourg at Reading. Come the end of the season, England manager Kevin Keegan gave Gerrard the first of his 114 caps against Ukraine at Wembley on the day after his 20th birthday.

The season saw Steven on a learning curve. Houllier didn't start Gerrard for the derby with Everton at Anfield, going for the experience of Didi Hamann, but when Gerrard was unleashed from the bench he was so fired up to impress he was sent off for a foul and duly suspended for three games. He was a quick learner thankfully and came back seemingly mentally stronger and learning to cope with the pressures of top-level football. 1999-2000 would go down as a less than memorable season by Liverpool's standards. Despite being runners-up in the league they were way behind the champions Manchester United and made no notable impression in the cups. However, Houllier was developing a side in which Stevie G was key and twelve months on, both domestic cups and a European trophy would be requiring the Anfield cleaners to dig out the silver polish!

The arrival of Sami Hyypiä stiffened the defence. The famous Finn had been recommended to the club by a TV cameraman who covered matches in the Netherlands where Hyypiä was playing. Not every club listens to its fans as Liverpool do but the Reds checked Sami out, loved what they saw and signed a player who would become a legend. 1999-2000 would be Hyypiä's first season. He would be ever-present and a major reason Liverpool had the best defence in the Premier League at the time.

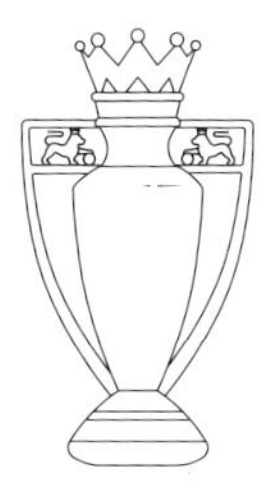

4TH

Liverpool ended with 67 points, two points behind Leeds.

4TH ROUND

Liverpool beat Huddersfield to make the 4th round.

3RD ROUND

Liverpool beat Hull 9-3 on aggregate in round two.

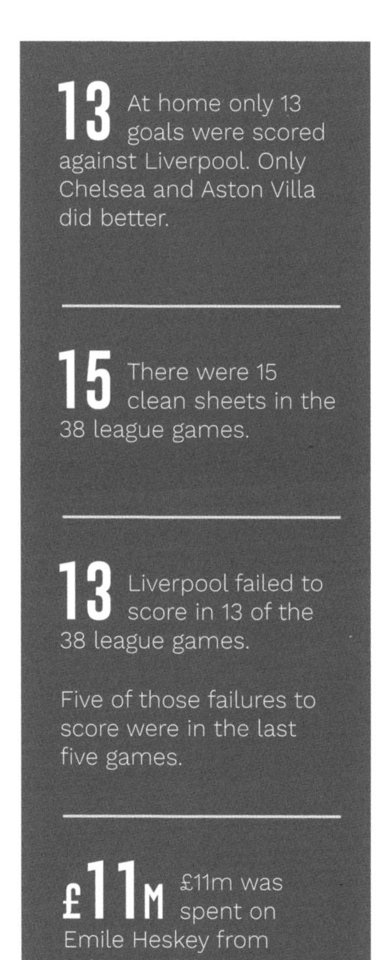

13 At home only 13 goals were scored against Liverpool. Only Chelsea and Aston Villa did better.

15 There were 15 clean sheets in the 38 league games.

13 Liverpool failed to score in 13 of the 38 league games.

Five of those failures to score were in the last five games.

£11M £11m was spent on Emile Heskey from Leicester City.

AVERAGE HOME LEAGUE ATTENDANCE

44,074

HIGHEST ATTENDANCE

44,929

VS MANCHESTER UNITED

LOWEST ATTENDANCE

40,483

VS BRADFORD CITY

GÉRARD HOULLIER

MICHAEL OWEN

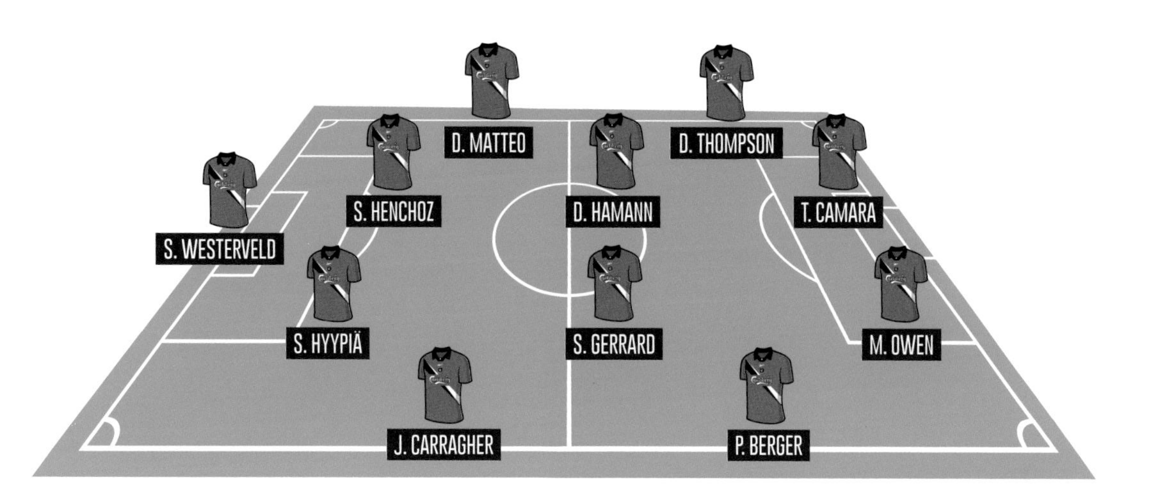

2005-06 AWAY

Made by Reebok in the last year that they produced Liverpool kits (to date), the 2005-06 away kit was similar to that worn in 2003-04, 1998-99, 1986-87 and in turn to the regular white shirt and black shorts often worn as an away outfit at times throughout history right back to the club's very early days.

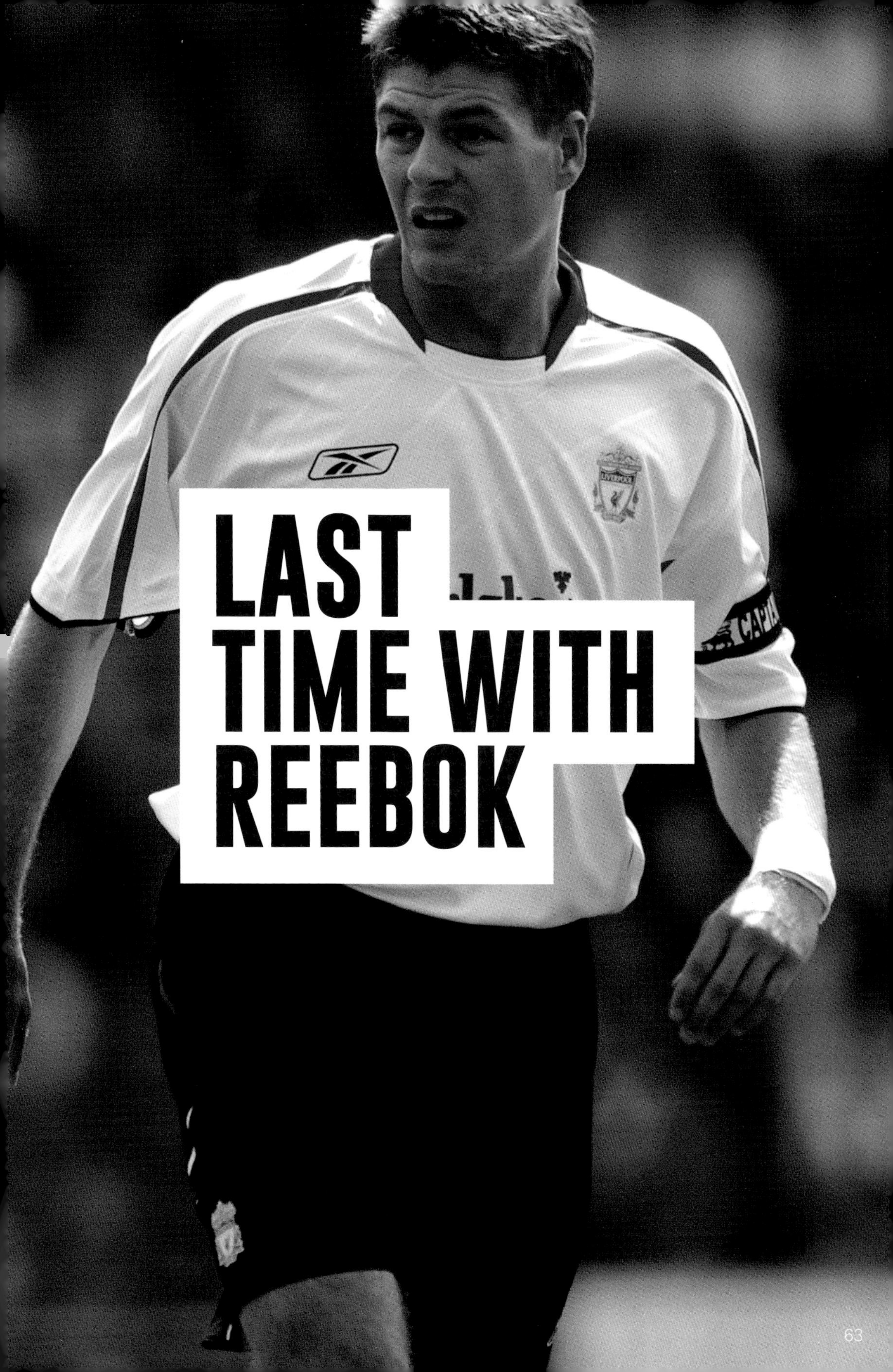

LAST TIME WITH REEBOK

A white away shirt kept the club colour of red alive with attractive red trimmings on the collar, and a thin red stripe on the sleeves and each side of the body of the shirt. The single curved stripe down each side helped to frame the sponsor name of the brewers Carlsberg which was in green, as was the top and bottom of the club badge. There was also a little bit of black for the manufacturer's logo and a thin edge on the end of the shirt sleeves, with black also employed on the back for the name and number.

Matched with black shorts and white socks with black and white tops and the letters L.F.C. in black on the shin, it was a relatively simple kit which varied slightly from competition to competition with the relevant competition sleeve badges. Sponsorship regulations in Under-18 games also meant the shirt was worn minus the Carlsberg logo at those fixtures.

The FA Cup and UEFA Super Cup came to Anfield with the final of the FIFA Club World Cup reached. West Ham were beaten on penalties in the last FA Cup final to be staged at Cardiff's Millennium Stadium. In what became known as the Gerrard final, Liverpool came from 2-0 and 3-2 down, with the second of Stevie G's braces coming in injury time before the legendary Liverpool number eight also scored in a penalty shoot-out. Keeper Pepe Reina saved three of the four penalties he faced to secure the trophy.

Djibril Cissé was always a man for the big occasion. He scored Liverpool's first goal in the FA Cup final and had netted twice at the start of the season as CSKA Moscow were defeated 3-1 in the UEFA Super Cup after extra time in Monaco.

December brought a trip to Japan for the FIFA Club World Cup where Costa Rican club Deportivo Saprissa were taken care of in the semi-final before a 1-0 defeat was suffered to São Paulo of Brazil, despite Liverpool dominating most of the match.

Liverpool had qualified for both the Super Cup and Club World Cup by being Champions League holders. The defence of the trophy began well with a group - that included Chelsea - won without defeat and only one goal conceded. Once into the round of 16 though, Liverpool lost both legs without scoring against Benfica.

In the Premier League, too many draws early on meant the Reds spent the first part of the season hovering half-way down the table, until a splendid ten-game winning run lifted Liverpool to third. Then, however, a run of just one point from four games undid the good work with third position unable to be improved on despite ending the campaign on a nine-game winning run.

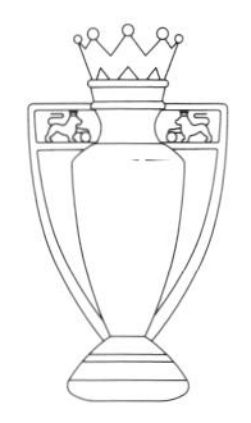

AVERAGE HOME LEAGUE ATTENDANCE

44,236

HIGHEST ATTENDANCE
44,983 VS TOTTENHAM HOTSPUR

LOWEST ATTENDANCE
42,293 VS FULHAM

3R
Finishing one point behind rivals Manchester United.

WINNERS
3-1 on penalties against West Ham.

3RD ROUND
2-1 defeat to Crystal Palace.

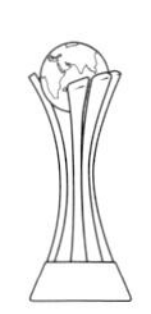

RAFA BENÍTEZ

RUNNERS-UP
Final taking place in Yokohama.

LAST 16
Biggest win coming in the group stage against Anderlecht, 3-0 at home.

WINNERS
García with an extra time goal to secure the silverware.

59 Sami Hyypiä played in 59 of the season's 63 games.

Nine men played in 50 or more matches.

£6.9M £6.9m spent on Spanish Goalkeeper Pepe Reina from Villarreal.

1-0 Liverpool lost the final of the FIFA Club World Cup 1-0 despite having 17 corners to São Paulo's none.

10 Four players scored over 10 goals.

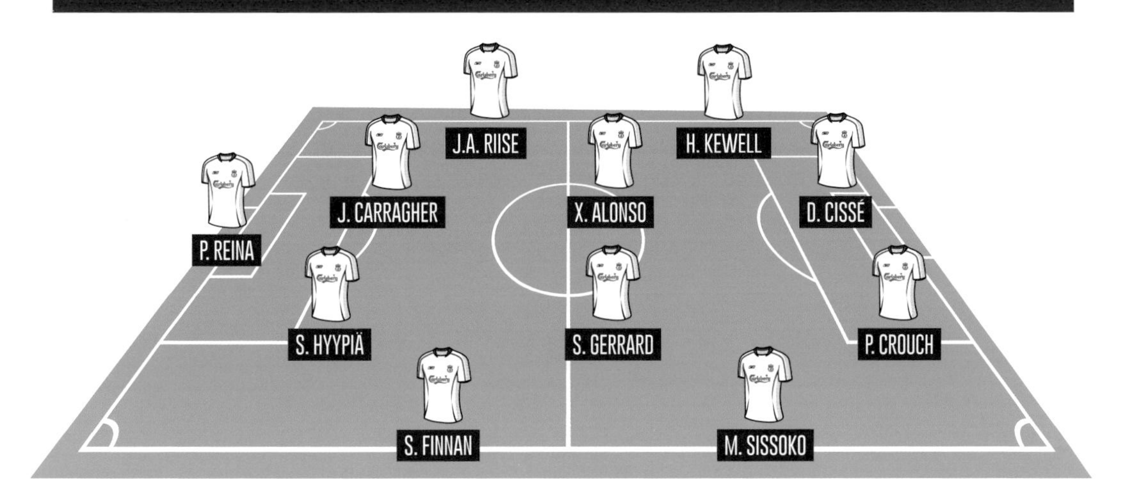

2008-09 AWAY

Produced by Adidas, Liverpool's away kit for 2008-09 consisted of an all-grey uniform. The shirt had a central red Adidas logo just below a circular collar. The club badge was in its usual place on the left side of the chest with a prominent Carlsberg sponsor logo in white; the same colour used for the player name and number on the back.

AN ALL GREY NOD

As always with Adidas there were three stripes on the sleeves. These stopped just above the sleeve patches, indicating the relevant tournament being played in. There was also a sliver of red on the very ends of the sleeves.

Combined with grey shorts and socks, all accompanied by the usual Adidas branding, it was a plain but dull kit; another to add to the list of strips that were arguably better suited – in terms of the tops at least – to leisurewear rather than actually playing football in. Bear in mind the fuss made when Manchester United infamously wore grey and had to change to a blue and white kit at half time after claims that players struggled to pick each other out against the crowd at Southampton in 1996.

While interest in the domestic cups ended early, Liverpool were runners-up in the Premier League for the first time since 2002 and had a decent run in the Champions League, before disappointingly coming unstuck against Chelsea.

Unbeaten in topping a group that included Atlético Madrid, Rafa Benítez's side beat Real Madrid 5-0 on aggregate in the round of 16 but (despite being unbeaten at home all season in the Premier League) lost 1-3 at home in the quarter-final to Chelsea. That left them needing to go to Stamford Bridge and emulate October's Premier League win there, when the Reds ended the Blues' 86-game unbeaten home Premier League record. For a while it looked as if a repeat might be on when Fabio Aurelio's free kick and Xabi Alonso's penalty drew the score level on aggregate, even if Chelsea still had an away goal advantage. Chelsea, though, fought back to lead 3-2 on the night but in a classic match, Lucas Leiva and Dirk Kuyt both found the back of the net to bring the score to 4-3 to Liverpool and 6-5 to Chelsea on aggregate. Another goal for Liverpool would give the Merseysiders the advantage on away goals - only for Frank Lampard's second goal of the match to level on the night and knock Liverpool out. Steven Gerrard sadly missed this game through injury, otherwise maybe Liverpool would have progressed to a semi-final with Barcelona.

Liverpool finished three points ahead of Chelsea in the Premier League but four points behind champions Manchester United. For much of the first half of the season, Liverpool topped the table and, while in the final analysis they remained unable to deliver a first Premier League Title, there was clear evidence that they were improving and narrowing the gap to what it took to take the title.

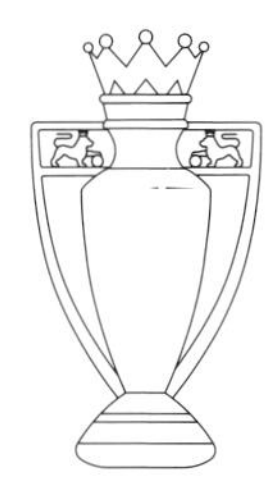

RUNNERS-UP

Four points behind winners Manchester United.

4TH ROUND

1-0 away defeat to city rivals Everton.

4TH ROUND

Tottenham getting the better on the day winning 4-2.

QTR-FINALS

Liverpool finished top of their group with 14 points, winning 4 drawing 2.

54 Jamie Carragher was the highest appearance maker, playing in 54 games.

Pepe Reina and Dirk Kuyt also played over 50 times.

Defeat at home to Chelsea in the Champions League was Liverpool's first home defeat in a first-leg tie in Europe since losing to Leeds in the 1970-71 Inter-Cities Fairs Cup semi-final first leg.

12 In addition to his 24 goals Stevie G topped the assists chart with 12.

AVERAGE HOME LEAGUE ATTENDANCE
43,611

HIGHEST ATTENDANCE
44,424 VS ARSENAL

LOWEST ATTENDANCE
41,169 VS WEST HAM UNITED

RAFA BENÍTEZ

STEVEN GERRARD

2014-15 AWAY

Although the away kit for 2014-15 was yellow, the eye was drawn to the red in the strip. From shoulder to shoulder under the collar but above the club and manufacturer's logo, a swirling red line made for an attractive design.

OLD CLASSIC RE-WORKED

Combined with the red on the Standard Chartered name and logo allied to the plain red liver bird badge and Warrior company logo, the clear red synonymous with Liverpool was evident within the yellow base colour. A red stripe down the side and on the edge of the end of the sleeves completed the look.

Although basically an all-yellow top, the reverse of the shirt saw the swirling red line continue to encase the shoulder and armpit area on both sides with the name and number in red, creating more of a yellow and red look.

In marketing material, a yellow line on the yellow shorts theoretically carried on the line on the shirts although in practice the shorts didn't often line up perfectly with the shirts. Completing the all-yellow outfit, a red hoop and red L.F.C. letters decorated the yellow socks.

From only their second game onwards, Liverpool never broke into the top four all season and on a couple of occasions even dropped into the bottom half. For the last few weeks Brendan Rodgers' side stayed in fifth place, but five losses in the last nine games saw a final placing of sixth. There had also been six defeats in the opening 12 games, so the start and end to the campaign was nowhere near good enough. This was especially the case when they astonishingly crumbled to an embarrassing final day 6-1 defeat at Stoke City in what was Steven Gerrard's final game. In the middle section of the season, twelve wins, four draws and just a solitary defeat meant that Liverpool looked much more like the level expected.

Decent runs in both domestic cups came to an end at the semi-final stage. In the FA Cup Liverpool were held to goalless draws at Anfield by both Bolton and Blackburn, with every round being won away from home until defeat was inflicted by Aston Villa. The League Cup saw a similar pattern. In three home games only a 2-1 victory over Swansea brought a straightforward victory; penalties being needed to defeat Middlesbrough while Chelsea took home a semi-final draw before beating the Reds at Stamford Bridge.

In Europe Liverpool could only finish third in their Champions League group, behind Basel as well as Real Madrid. Demoted to the Europa League it was then Liverpool's turn to lose on penalties, going out to Beşiktaş at the first hurdle after entering the competition.

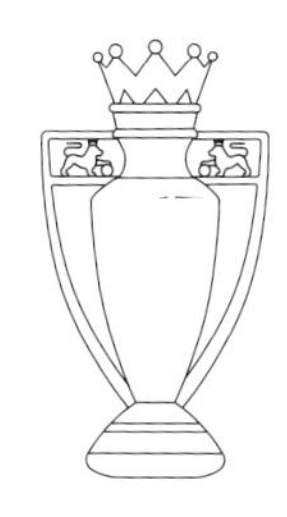

6TH

8 points behind winners Manchester United.

SEMI-FINALS

A 14-13 FA Cup penalty shoot-out win over Middlesbrough was the joint highest scoring shoot-out in professional football in England.

SEMI-FINALS

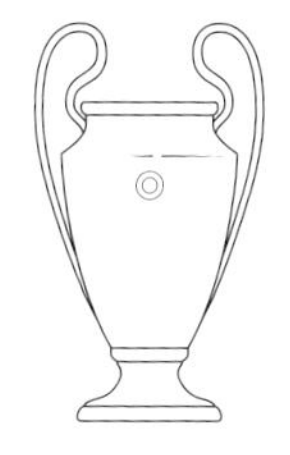

LAST 32

Liverpool suffered a 3-0 home defeat to Real Madrid in the group stage.

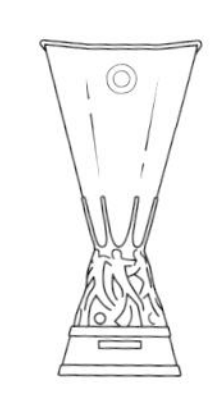

LAST 32

Sevilla won the Europa League.

13 13 goals for the top scorer was the lowest since 2004-05 when this season's top scorer Steven Gerrard was one of three men to score 13 goals.

Philippe Coutinho was the Player of the Year and Players' Player of the Year as well as scoring the goal of the season against Southampton.

50 Jordan Henderson and Simon Mignolet were the only players to make over 50 appearances.

6-1 Steven Gerrard scored in his farewell game – but Liverpool lost 6-1.

That last day loss at Stoke was the first time Liverpool had conceded six in the league for 52 years.

BRENDAN RODGERS

STEVEN GERRARD

AVERAGE HOME LEAGUE ATTENDANCE

44,659

HIGHEST ATTENDANCE

44,736 VS SOUTHAMPTON

LOWEST ATTENDANCE

44,405 VS MAN UNITED

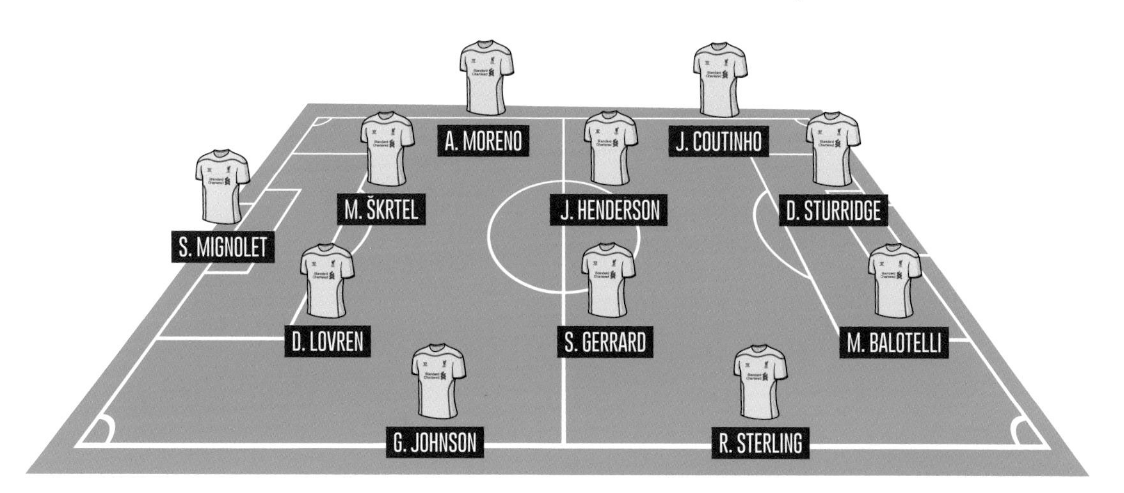

2017-18 AWAY

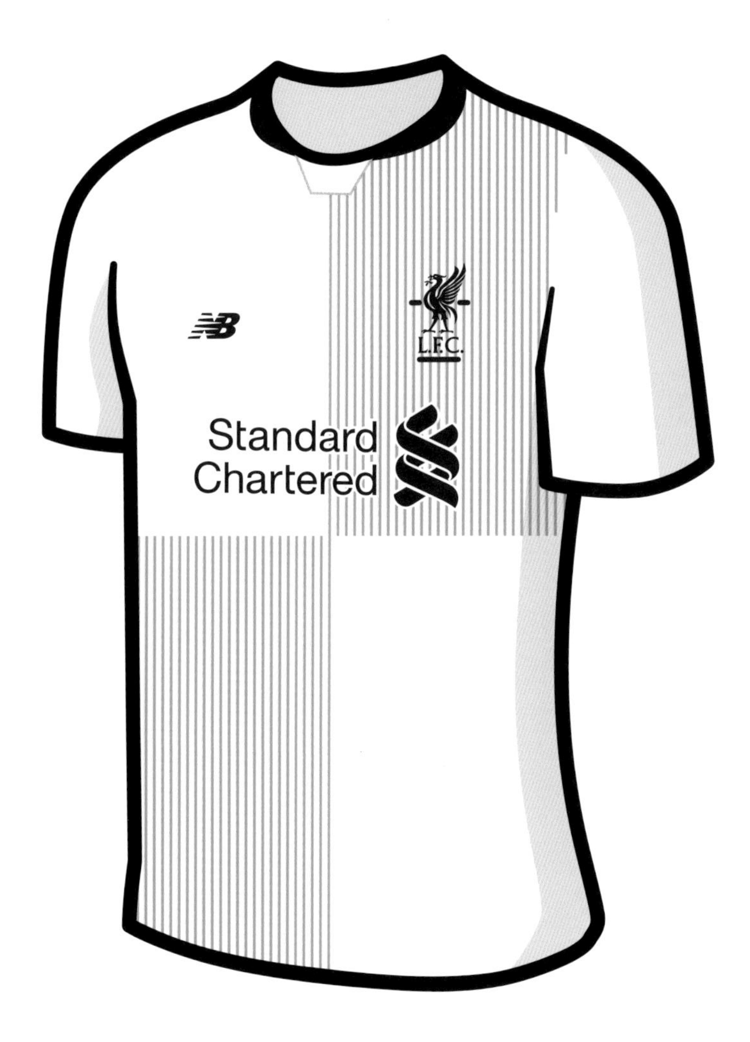

In a radical departure from tradition, a quartered away shirt was introduced by New Balance for 2017-18. In English football, quartered shirts are most associated with the blue and white quarters of Bristol Rovers, but Liverpool's shirt did not possess the bold primary colour of the Pirates. Instead the thin green and white striped quarters used alongside two white quarters looked rather like the colour someone might turn if told to walk the plank.

RETURN TO GREEN QUARTERS

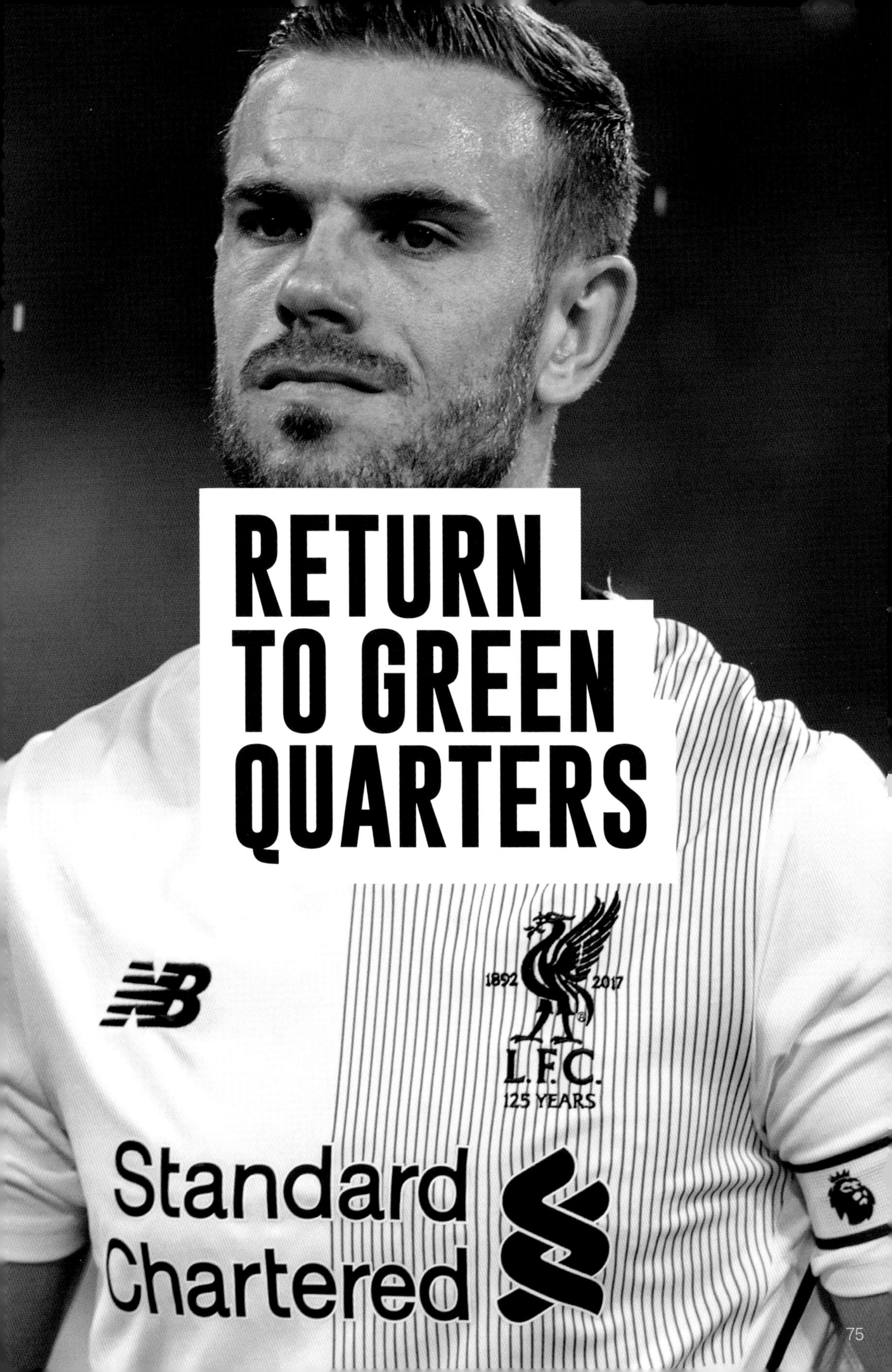

It really was an insipid looking shirt. It did not signal strength and that was matched in too many weak performances as Liverpool endured a disappointing season. Black was used for the shirt's trimmings: the Standard Chartered sponsor, the collar and New Balance logo. The club badge was simply a black liver bird with the numbers 1892 and 2017 while underneath the liver bird was 'L.F.C. 125 years', also in black. The quartered look was only used on the front, with the back a plain white other than for the player name and number in black.

The strip was completed by black shorts and white socks. The socks had black tops and in the middle of the shin a green band which contained the letters L.F.C. in white.

An initial fee of £36.5m for an ex-Chelsea forward who had scored just twice in 13 league games for the Blues before being twice loaned out did not look to be the most exciting of record buys when Liverpool brought in an Egyptian forward from Roma. That player, of course, was Mo Salah who has proved to be one of the most exciting players Anfield has seen and a candidate for inclusion in an all-time XI.

A scorer on his Premier League debut at Watford, Salah became the man of the 'Mo-ment' as he took Anfield by storm. He scored in 24 of the 36 Premier League games he played in his first season, totalling 44 goals in all. It made Salah the country's top scorer in a campaign in which he was Premier League Player of the Month three times and scored four times in a 5-0 home win over Watford.

Despite Salah's scoring, Liverpool could not get into the title race. From just before Christmas, they managed to maintain a top-four position, and in late February/early March they rose as high as second – but even then were a distant 15 points behind leaders Manchester City.

Only Everton were beaten as Liverpool suffered early exits in both domestic cups, but in the Champions League at least, Jürgen Klopp's side were at their best. 15 games were played as Liverpool reached the final with the terrific triumvirate of Salah, Sadio Mané and Roberto Firmino all reaching double figures in Champions League goals alone. Manchester City may have been convincing Premier League champions but had no answer to Liverpool's European know-how as the Reds beat them home and away in the quarter-final. While Roma threatened a second-leg comeback after losing 5-2 at Anfield in the semi-final, Liverpool marched into the final for a classic clash with Real Madrid. Unfortunately a calamitous performance by goalkeeper Loris Karius, combined with a stellar display by Real's Gareth Bale, meant that Liverpool lost the show-piece game 3-1.

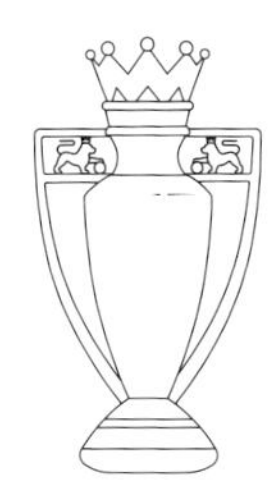

4TH

There were 17 Premier League clean sheets.

4TH ROUND

3-2 defeat to West Brom.

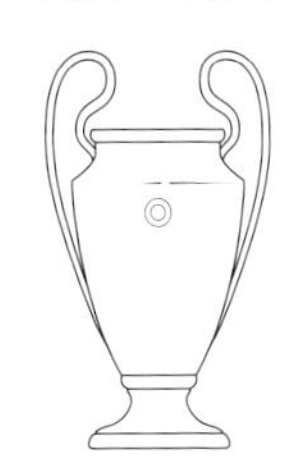

3RD ROUND

Leicester City coming out on top with a 2-0 win.

RUNNERS-UP

7-0 against Spartak Moscow, was the biggest home win in the Champions League.

94 With 44 goals in 4,116 minutes play, Salah scored the equivalent of once every 94 minutes.

50 Roberto Firmino, Mo Salah and Georginio Wijnaldum all made at least 50 appearances.

26 26 of Liverpool's 56 games featured at least four goals.

Goal of the Season: Alex Oxlade-Chamberlain (vs. Manchester City, 4 April 2018).

18 18 different players scored for Liverpool – plus three own goals.

30 Firmino and Salah contributed 30 assists between them.

JÜRGEN KLOPP

MO SALAH

AVERAGE HOME LEAGUE ATTENDANCE

53,059

HIGHEST ATTENDANCE

53,287

VS NEWCASTLE AND WATFORD

LOWEST ATTENDANCE

50,752

VS BRIGHTON & HOVE ALBION

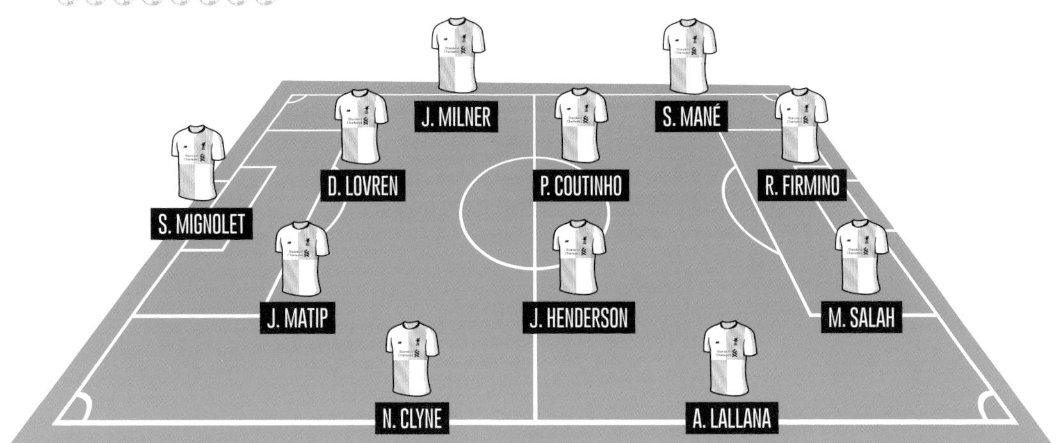

2020-21 AWAY

Critics of the 2020-21 kit thought the absence of fans was the only excuse for Liverpool to wear the season's away strip - but on the other hand, dedicated followers of fashion loved it.

FOR THE FASHION FOLLOWERS

Made by Nike, it came with the usual marketing jargon concerning a Nike Breathe fabric incorporating Dri-Fit technology. The all-over print looked something like a stormy sea – perhaps the designers had taken the words 'When you walk through a storm' from 'You'll Never Walk Alone' literally.

Officially described as teal and black the shirt was inspired by the liver bird and Shankly Gates, with the base teal colour of the shirt and shorts featuring a swirling overlay. The collar was a crew-neck in contrast to the V-neck of that season's home and third shirts.

Black was used for the neck, sleeve edges, name, number, sponsor name, Nike swoosh and club badge. It was also used for a 'Justice for the 96' emblem below the nape of the neck.

With the shorts and socks also in teal, the strip was undoubtedly eye-catchingly attractive and instantly visible from an on-field playing perspective. "We have very distinct design filters that are fully demonstrated in the collection we have created for Liverpool" said Scott Munson, VP football apparel representative at Nike. He continued, "First and foremost we set out to create a collection that celebrates the rich culture of the city of Liverpool and the club. The away kit allowed us to be bolder and more expressive in how we brought some of these cultural references to life and we've landed on a look and aesthetic that really reflects that."

For the last two weeks of 2020, Liverpool led the table as they looked to defend their first ever Premier League Title. This run included a stunning 7-0 win at Crystal Palace, against a team managed by former Liverpool boss Roy Hodgson. That result established a healthy five-point lead at the top of the league.

After losing to Arsenal on penalties in the Community Shield, the season started with three wins including victories at Chelsea and at home to the Gunners. Then came the sensational shock of a stunning 7-2 defeat at Aston Villa. It was the first time the league's reigning champions had conceded seven goals since Arsenal did so at Sunderland in 1953. The result at Villa Park also meant that Liverpool had leaked 11 goals in their first four league games for the first time since 1937-38. After an international break to digest that defeat, the Reds returned at Goodison Park where they were held to a 2-2 draw by Everton, but they then got into their stride with 10 points from the next four games, the only draw being a creditable one at Manchester City. That sequence was the start of a 12-game unbeaten run that took the team up to the end of the calendar year (and included the 7-0 win at Crystal Palace).

2021 was to see a bigger shock than that bad result at Villa: having gone a record 68 home league games without defeat, Burnley, Brighton, Manchester City, Everton, Chelsea and Fulham managed to then inflict six incredible successive home losses on the Reds. By this time Jürgen Klopp's men had lost more home games than anyone outside the bottom three and had dropped to eighth. They were also completely out of the title race, being 22 points behind leaders Manchester City with 10 games left. No doubt the absence of supporters due to games being played behind closed doors because of the Covid 19 pandemic played an influential part in Anfield's fortress being stormed.

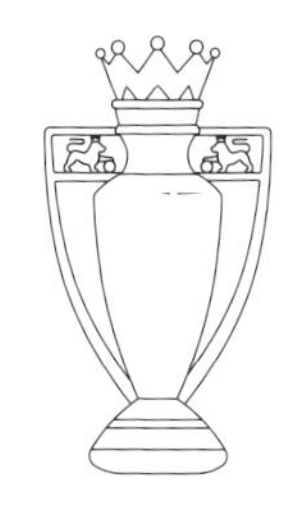

3RD

Goalkeeper Alisson scored his first for Liverpool.

4TH ROUND

3-2 defeat against Manchester United.

4TH ROUND

Arsenal advanced 5-4 on penalties.

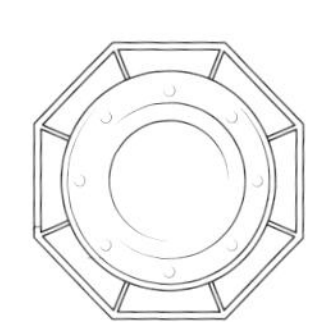

RUNNERS-UP

Arsenal won 5-4 on penalties... again!

QTR-FINALS

Liverpool's biggest win coming from a 5-0 thrashing of Atalanta.

JÜRGEN KLOPP

MO SALAH

AVERAGE HOME LEAGUE ATTENDANCE 836*

HIGHEST ATTENDANCE
9,901 VS CRYSTAL PALACE*

LOWEST ATTENDANCE
0 VS 15 OPPONENTS*

*The attendance figures were affected by Covid

68 The club's longest ever unbeaten home league record of 68 games without defeat ended with a loss to Burnley on 21st January 2021.

Amazingly the loss to Burnley was the first of six successive home defeats.

In December Jürgen Klopp was named FIFA men's Coach of the Year for 2020.

Alisson's last-minute winner against West Brom was the first ever goal scored by a Liverpool goalkeeper.

The goal – which helped Liverpool qualify for the Champions League – was named Goal of the Season.

127 The 7-0 win at Palace saw Jürgen Klopp overtake Rafa Benítez with most Premier League wins - 127.

TH

RD

1998-99 THIRD

A bright yellow shirt trimmed in red and black on the cuffs and collar was a basic but attractive top.

Other than the essential club badge and manufacturer's logo in red, Premier League badges on the sleeves and sponsor Carlsberg's name in black, the shirt was simplicity itself.

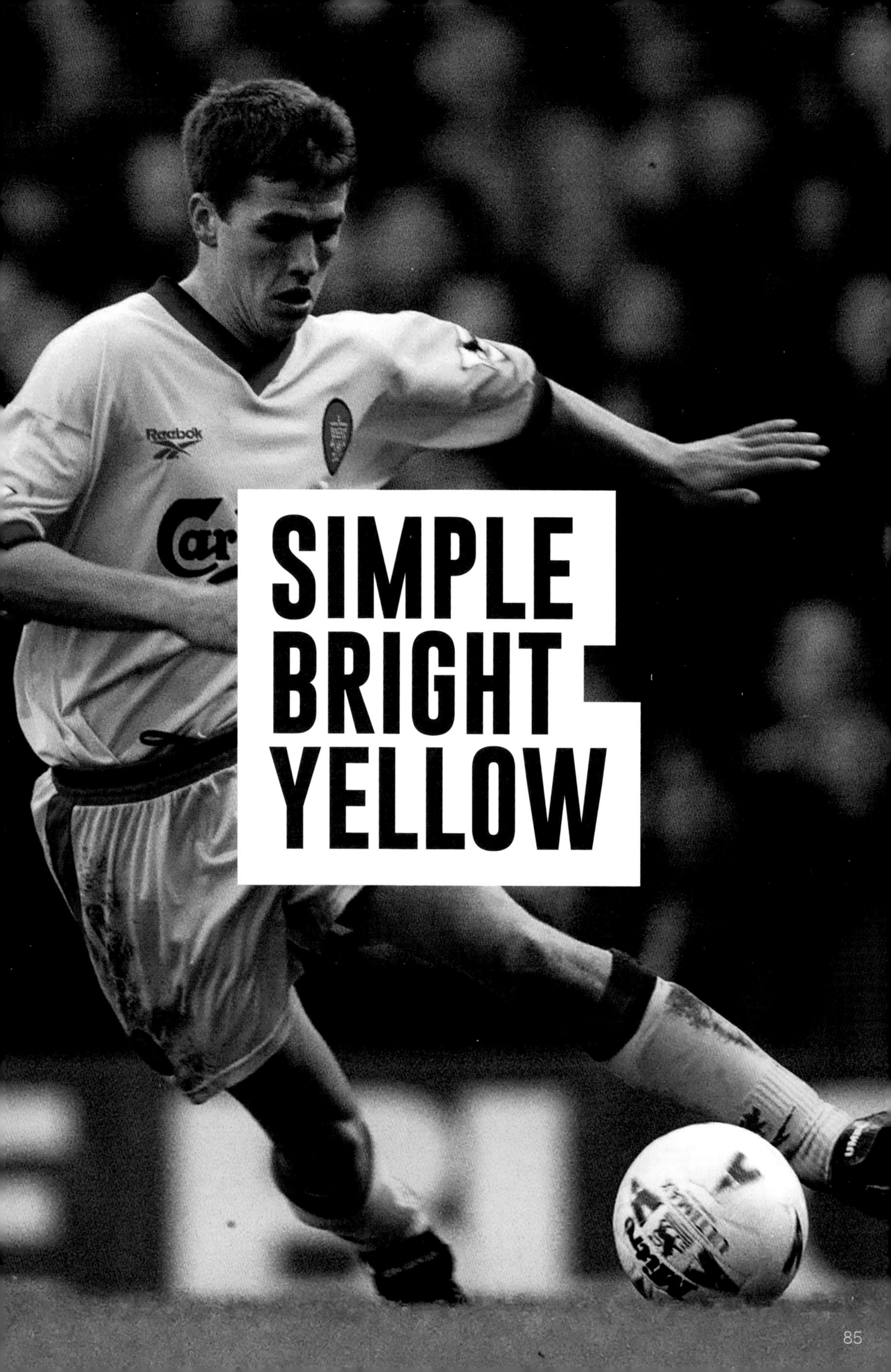

SIMPLE BRIGHT YELLOW

The kit was completed with yellow shorts and socks, both complemented by red trimmings. In the case of the shorts this involved a red stripe down the side with red used for the Reebok logo and club badge, while the socks had red tops above a red liver bird on the shin above a black Reebok logo.

Having brought in former France manager Gérard Houllier to work alongside Roy Evans, Liverpool started the season with two managers, but by mid-November Evans resigned, stepping aside to leave Houllier in sole charge. Evans wasn't the only big name to depart. Star man Steve McManaman left in one of the early 'Bosman' frees to Real Madrid; the England international exercising his right to move on at the end of his contract without Liverpool being able to command a fee for one of the continent's top talents.

It was a poor season for Anfield regulars. Early elimination from all three cup competitions and a disappointing seventh-place finish in the Premier League, the lowest in five years. There had been early hope of a title challenge when the table was topped after the first four games, but by mid-December they had slumped to 12th place and by April were still languishing in 10th spot. As the dust settled on the season, the realisation dawned that the following term would be the first in five years without European competition to look forward to.

In a season of transition no-one played in more than 34 of the 38 Premier League games; Jamie Carragher, Paul Ince, Jamie Redknapp and Karl-Heinz Riedle being the quartet to play in all but four games. In all competitions seven players made 40 or more appearances, Carragher topping the list with 44 outings.

To commemorate the 100th season of the Football League, Liverpool ended the season with a 3-2 win at Sunderland in a challenge match between Liverpool (the team to win the league the most times) and the Wearsiders (who had just won the Football League with a record 105 points).

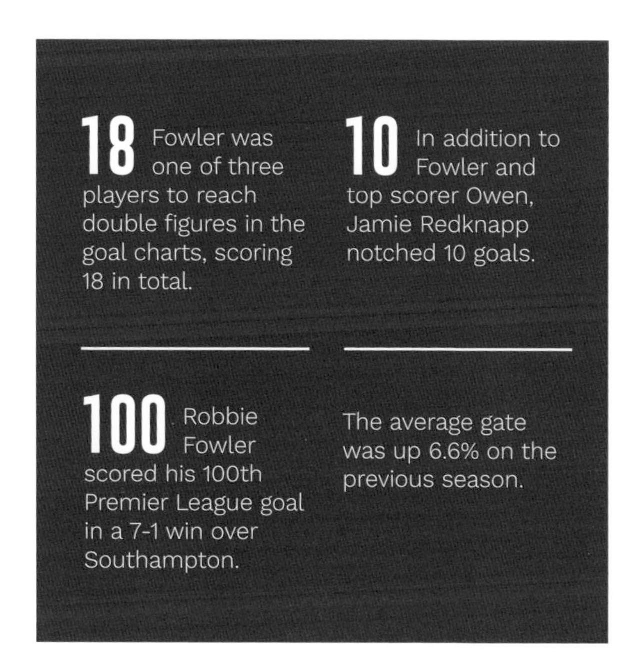

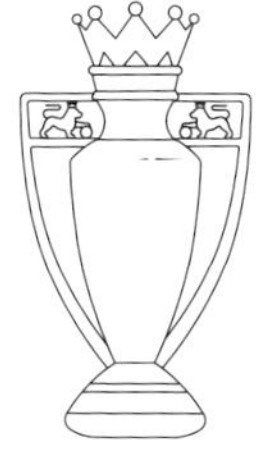

7TH

One point behind Aston Villa and two ahead of Derby County.

4TH ROUND

Eliminated 2-1 against Manchester United.

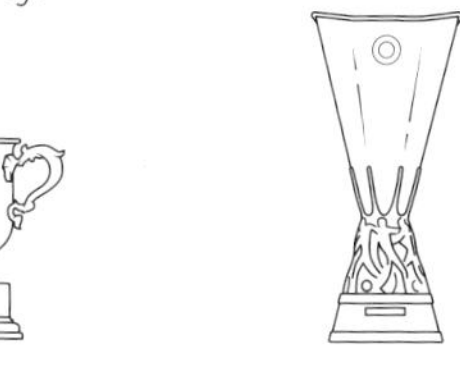

3RD ROUND

A 3-1 defeat against Tottenham.

3RD ROUND

Losing to Celta Vigo after beating Valencia and Košice.

AVERAGE HOME LEAGUE ATTENDANCE 43,321

HIGHEST ATTENDANCE 44,852

VS EVERTON

LOWEST ATTENDANCE 36,019

VS LEICESTER CITY

ROY EVANS & GÉRARD HOULLIER

Joint managers until the 12th of November with Houllier then sole manager.

MICHAEL OWEN

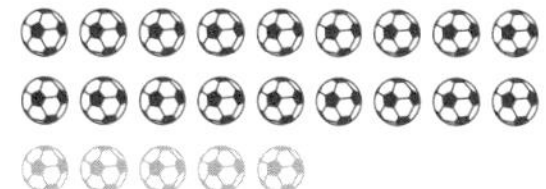

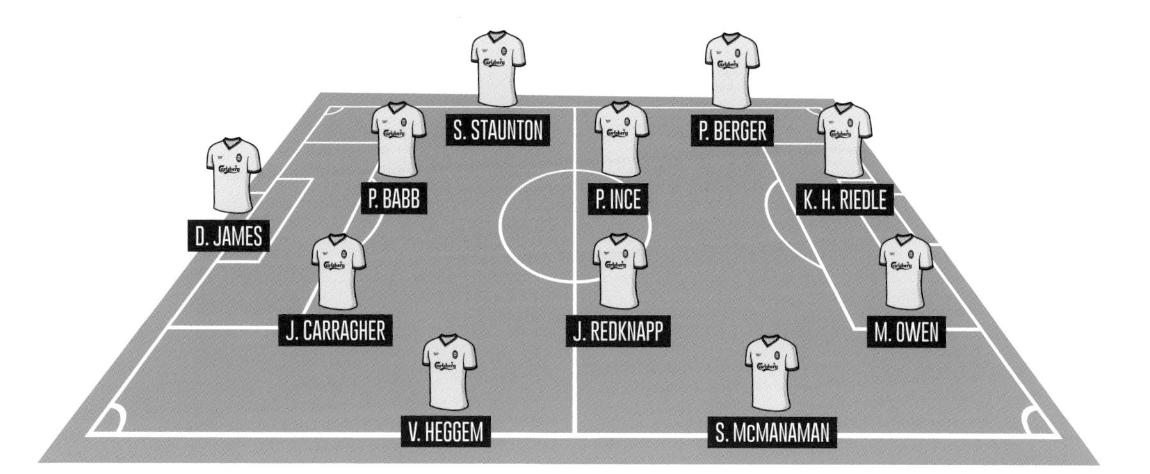

2001-02 THIRD

Yellow had long been seen as an alternative colour for the Reds, almost like adding custard to rhubarb! First seen in the fifties, yellow had been worn occasionally in the sixties but it was in the late seventies and especially the eighties that yellow was a colour Liverpool's away supporters could get used to seeing; most often as a third kit.

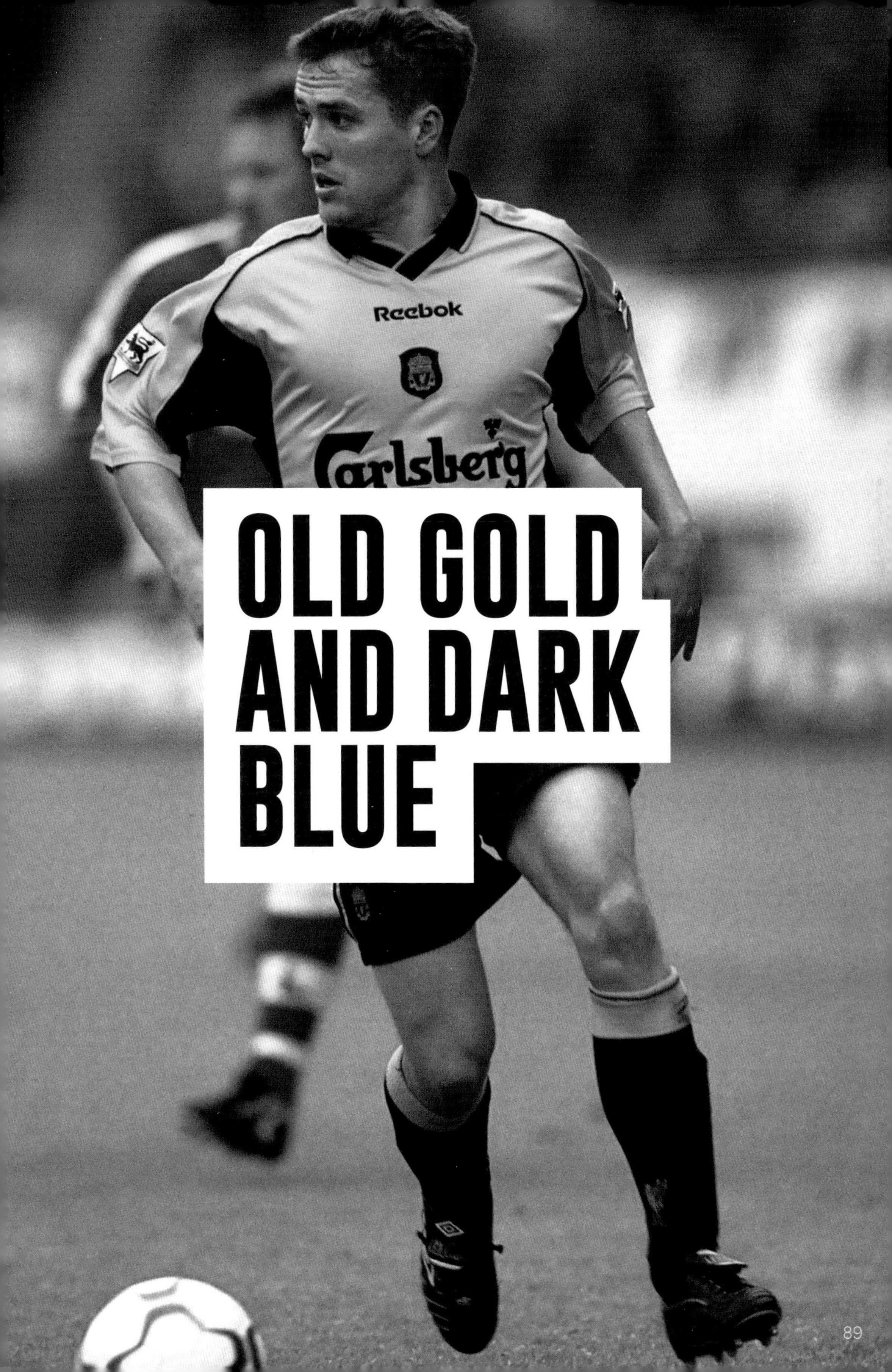

OLD GOLD AND DARK BLUE

The 'darker' (as opposed to bright) yellow used by Reebok as a third kit in 2001 appeared to be a similar shade to that used by Adidas on the third kit between 1994 and 1996.

Previously used as a first choice away kit in 2000-01 when it was worn in a victorious FA Cup final, the 2001-02 third kit shirt was paired with dark blue shorts sporting yellow stripes on the sides. The socks were the same dark blue with yellow tops that displayed a dark blue Reebok logo and the liver bird badge in yellow on the shins.

The shirt was a simple, almost Wolverhampton Wanderers-like 'old gold' yellow with very dark blue panels on the sides and the underneath of the sleeves. Beneath a dark blue collar edged in yellow, the manufacturer's name, club badge and Carlsberg sponsor name were all positioned centrally in that almost-black, extremely dark blue.

This wasn't as good a season as the one before and yet progress was made! Two trophies were won as opposed to three but the UEFA Super Cup and Charity Shield didn't quite match up to the FA Cup, League Cup and UEFA Cup of the previous season. On the other hand, a climb to second from third in the Premier League was Liverpool's best yet since the breakaway from the Football League and the gap to the champions was reduced to seven points from the previous season's eleven. Arsenal were the champions so in this 10th season of the Premier League, Liverpool finished above Manchester United for the first time.

Such progress was achieved despite being without manager Gérard Houllier for five months in the middle of the season as the French leader convalesced from a heart problem, during which time ex-Reds skipper Phil Thompson did a great job as caretaker. Long before he took ill, Houllier had taken his number of trophies in the calendar year to five - Manchester United and Bayern Munich being beaten in the Charity Shield (the last time it was contested before changing its name to the Community Shield) and the UEFA Super Cup. As UEFA Cup holders, Liverpool beat Bayern's Champions League winners but would eventually go out of their first season in the continent's top competition to German opposition in the shape of Bayer Leverkusen, losing on aggregate to a late goal from Brazilian defender Lucio in Germany.

Late goals also cost Liverpool a shock home League Cup defeat to Grimsby Town as the defence of both domestic trophies were over quickly – FA Cup defeat at Arsenal coming in a tempestuous match of three red cards, to Jamie Carragher and the Gunners' Martin Keown and goal-scorer Dennis Bergkamp.

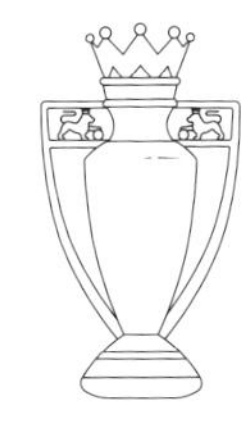

RUNNERS-UP

Liverpool spent three gameweeks at top spot during December.

3RD ROUND

A 2-1 loss to Grimsby Town.

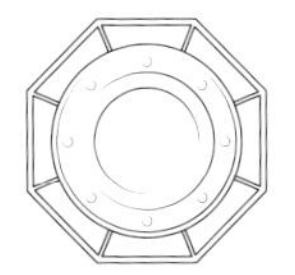

WINNERS

Beating Manchester United 2-1.

4TH ROUND

Knocked out away to Arsenal 1-0.

QTR-FINALS

Eliminated by finalists Bayer Leverkusen.

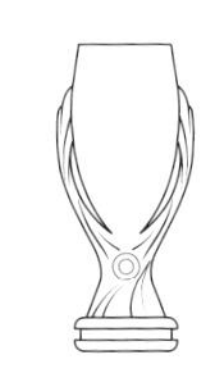

WINNERS

A 3-2 win over Bayern Munich in Monaco.

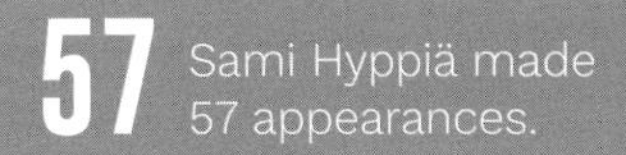

57 Sami Hyppiä made 57 appearances.

Stephane Henchoz, Emile Heskey, Danny Murphy and John Arne Riise each played 56 games.

12 Danny Murphy with 12 and Steven Gerrard with 11 were in double figures for assists.

14 Emile Heskey scored half as many as Michael Owen's total of 28 goals, but no-one else scored more than eight.

AVERAGE HOME LEAGUE ATTENDANCE

43,389

HIGHEST ATTENDANCE

44,371

VS EVERTON

LOWEST ATTENDANCE

37,163

VS FULHAM

GÉRARD HOULLIER

Phil Thompson was interim manager between 13th October, 2001 and 18th March, 2002.

MICHAEL OWEN

2004-05 THIRD

Made by Reebok, the kit used as a third choice outfit by Liverpool in 2004-05 had been the first choice away kit the previous season.

The shirt was a simple all-white with red and black trimmings. A single, predominantly red stripe down each side of the top brought a tinge of the traditional club colour to the white kit, while a stripe of the same colour appeared on the sleeves linked by the stripe continuing around the back of the neckline.

ALL WHITE WITH RED TRIMMINGS

Written in green, the name of sponsors Carlsberg stood out very clearly on the chest, with the club badge and Reebok logo neatly positioned above the sponsor name. Paired with black shorts showing the usual club badge and sponsor logo at the bottom of each leg, the kit was completed by white socks that featured black panels on the tops, framing the letters 'L.F.C.' and topped off by a horizontal red line.

A disappointing domestic season was more than outweighed by winning the Champions League in Istanbul. Liverpool trailed 3-0 at half time of the final following a first-minute goal by Paolo Maldini for AC Milan and two by Hernan Crespo shortly before the break. Lesser teams than Liverpool would have been well beaten at that stage, especially against a star-studded Milan line-up, but perhaps the greatest seven minutes in the history of the club began when Steven Gerrard pulled a goal back in the 54th minute. Two minutes later Vladimir Smicer made it 2-3 and Xabi Alonso completed the comeback on the hour mark. It was incredible stuff as Milan's seemingly unassailable lead was wiped out. After the equaliser caginess returned. An hour's further play, including extra-time, failed to produce another goal.

Inspired by his "inner Bruce Grobbelaar" - in the light of Liverpool's South African goalkeeper's successful antics in the 1984 European Cup final penalty shoot-out - Liverpool's Polish goalkeeper Jerzy Dudek successfully put off Milan's Serginho so that he missed the opening penalty kick to hand Benítez's men the advantage. When Dudek then saved Andrea Pirlo's penalty and Liverpool went 2-0 up, Liverpool looked as bound for success as Milan had been earlier. However, when John Arne Riise's penalty was saved after Jon Dahl Tomasson had made it 2-1, both sides then scored with their next attempts making it 3-2 to Liverpool after four penalties each. Milan had to score to keep the shoot-out alive and had one of the world's top strikers to take the pressure kick in Andrei Shevchenko. As the watching world held its breath, Dudek denied him as Liverpool completed an unbelievable comeback to become European champions for the first time since 1984.

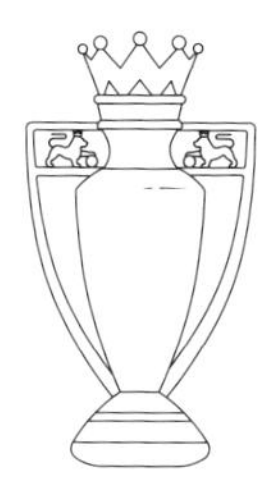

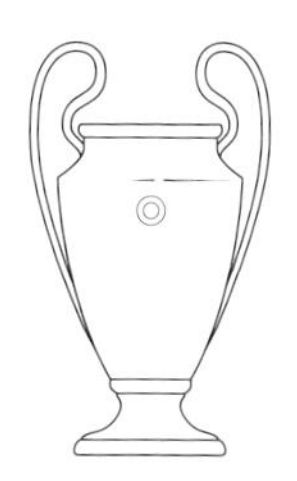

5TH
Level on points (58) with sixth place Bolton but with a higher goal difference.

3RD ROUND
Eliminated away to Burnley.

RUNNERS-UP
Beaten by Chelsea 3-2 after extra-time.

WINNERS
Winning on penalties after being 3-0 down at half time.

57 John Arne Riise was the highest appearance maker, playing 57 games.

Jamie Carragher and Steve Finnan also played over 50 games.

Riise created more goals than anyone else, assisting eight times.

8 Riise also scored eight goals.

£14.5M Djibril Cissé came in for £14.5m from Auxerre.

11 German midfielder Dietmar Hamann, accumulated 11 yellow cards over the season.

RAFA BENÍTEZ

MILAN BAROŠ
LUIS GARCÍA
STEVEN GERRARD

AVERAGE HOME LEAGUE ATTENDANCE 42,587

HIGHEST ATTENDANCE
44,224 VS EVERTON

LOWEST ATTENDANCE
35,064 VS PORTSMOUTH

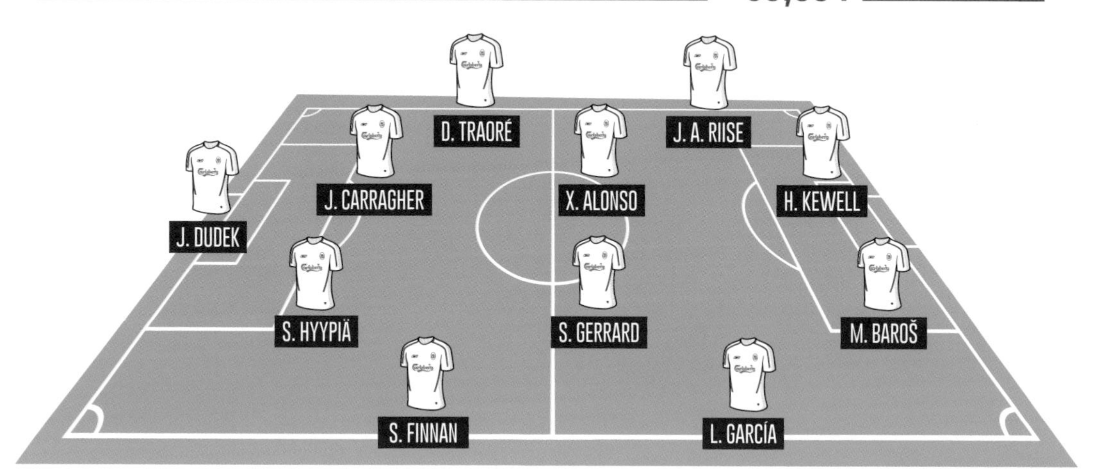

2006-07 THIRD

In this season's third kit, two team mates standing side by side but facing in opposite directions wouldn't necessarily look as if they were on the same team. This is because Liverpool's largely white third kit shirt had a huge chunk on the right-hand side that was dark green.

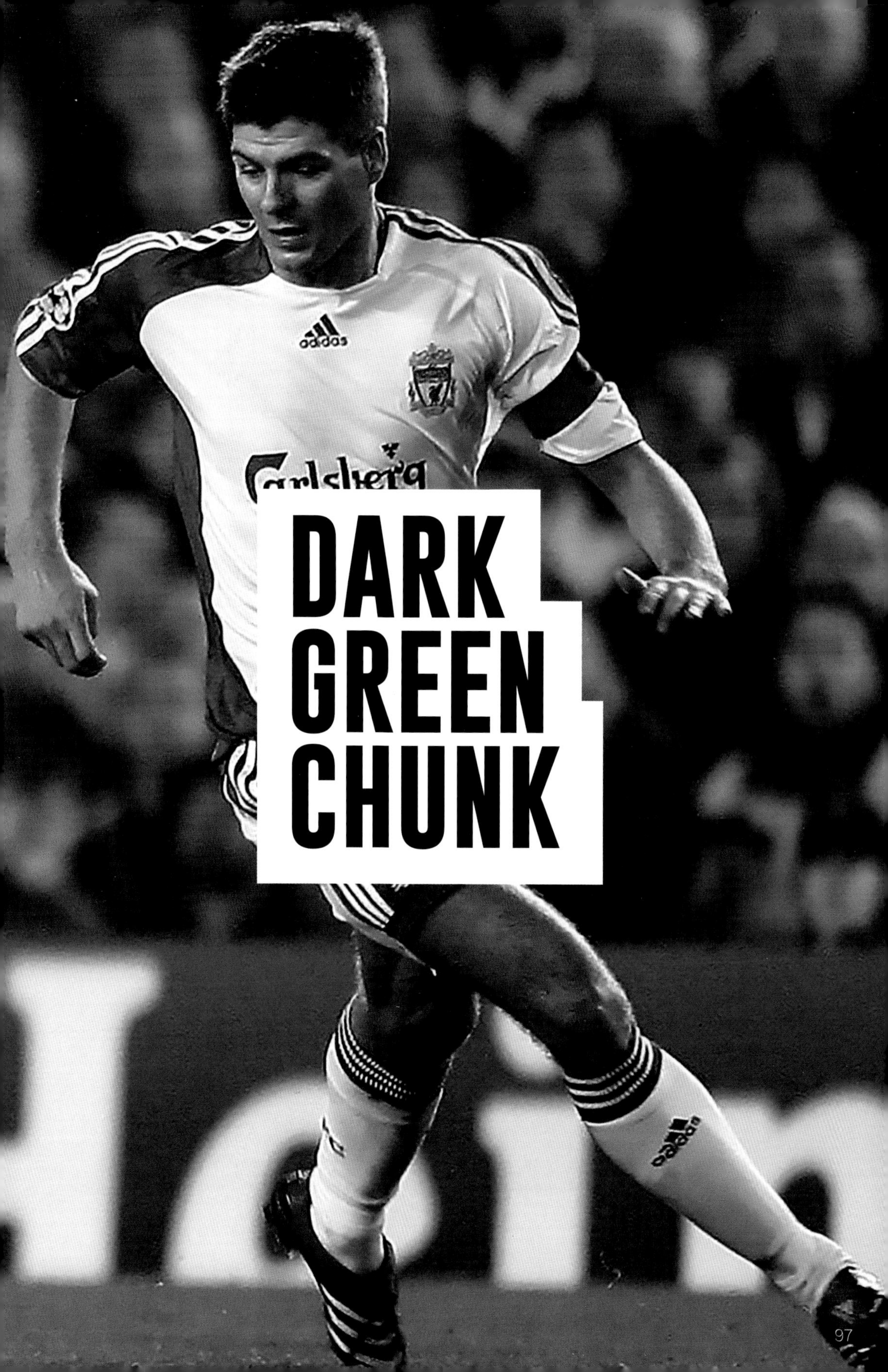
DARK
GREEN
CHUNK
adidas

Made by Adidas, the regular three Adidas stripes were in different colours on each sleeve: white on the green section of the shirt and green on the white part. Green was also used for the central Adidas badge and the Carlsberg sponsor logo, while the club badge was in red, white and green.

Similarly there was a large green area on the right-hand side of the otherwise white shorts. This green section encased the club badge while white socks were topped with green and white Celtic-like hoops along with a green Adidas logo in the centre of the shin. Perhaps surprisingly green was not used for the number and name on the back of the kit, red being used instead. As usual with the shirt sponsor being a brewer, kits worn in Under-18 games and for younger groups did not include the main sponsor.

After a slow start to the season in the Premier League, Liverpool spent almost all of the second half of the season in third place. After taking just one point from the final three games the Anfielders narrowly hung on to third spot, ahead of Arsenal on goal difference.

At home Liverpool were almost impregnable. Only seven goals were conceded at Anfield in the Premier League all season. No team came to the red side of Stanley Park and scored more than once in the league although that was sufficient for champions Manchester United to win 1-0. United's goal came after Liverpool kept nine successive home clean sheets.

In contrast, in the domestic cups Liverpool's rotated team conceded a lot of goals. Twelve were conceded in the three games played, with Arsenal netting nine of them! The Gunners astonishingly won 6-3 in the quarter-final of the League Cup and returned to win 3-1 in the FA Cup, although they were beaten 4-1 in a late season league visit. The Carling-sponsored League Cup also saw Reading come to Liverpool and score three in a seven-goal thriller.

There were also seven home games in the Champions League in which just five goals were conceded. Two of these were sufficient to taste defeat at the hands of Barcelona and Chelsea but Benítez's boys managed to progress despite both ties finishing level on aggregate. Having reached the final in Athens, Liverpool went down to two Filippo Inzaghi goals for AC Milan, with Dirk Kuyt's late goal proving to be no more than a small consolation.

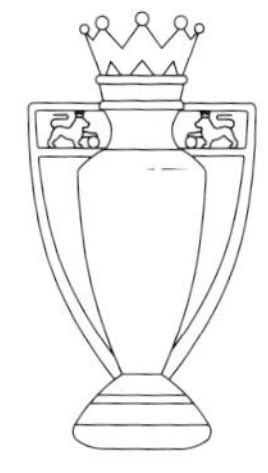

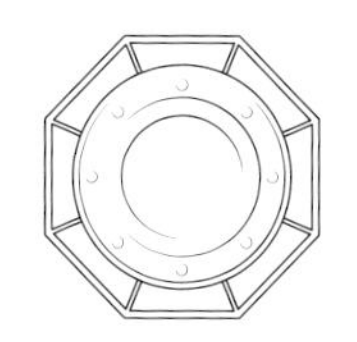

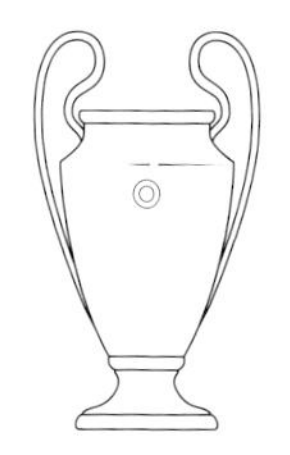

3RD

Liverpool had the league's tightest home defence.

3RD ROUND

54 of Liverpool's 111 goals came in cup games or the Community Shield.

QTR-FINALS

WINNERS

2-1 win over Chelsea.

RUNNERS-UP

Kuyt scored the only goal for Liverpool in a 2-1 defeat to AC Milan.

43 Peter Crouch, Dirk Kuyt and Steven Gerrard scored a combined 43 goals in all competitions.

10 No-one managed as many as 10 assists, Jermaine Pennant topping the list with nine.

Arsenal scored more cup goals at Anfield than were conceded at home all season in the Premier League.

Steven Gerrard was the fans' Player of the Year for a fourth successive season.

7 Liverpool were awarded seven Premier League penalties but only conceded one.

RAFA BENÍTEZ

PETER CROUCH

AVERAGE HOME LEAGUE ATTENDANCE **43,563**

HIGHEST ATTENDANCE 44,403 VS MAN UNITED

LOWEST ATTENDANCE 41,370 VS BOLTON WDR

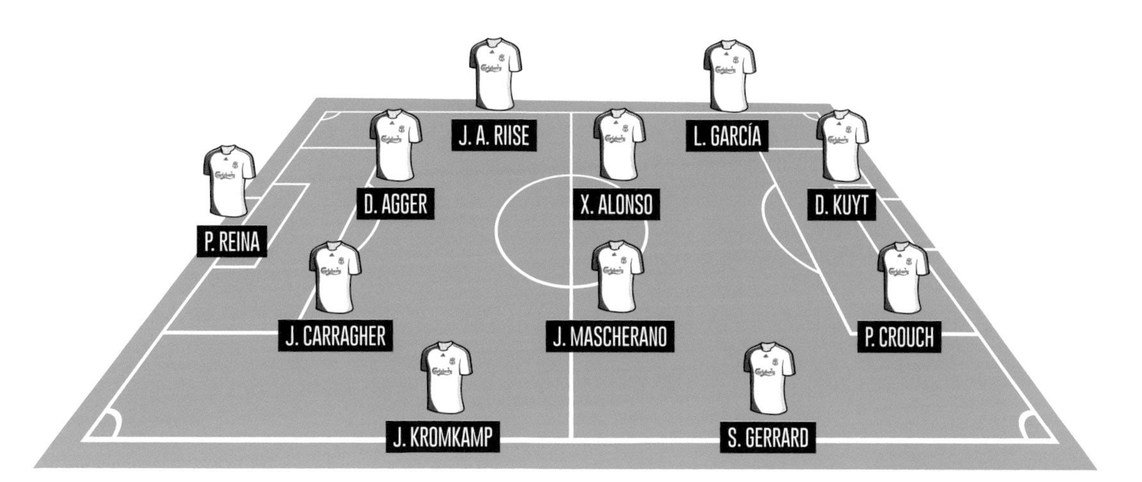

2011-12 THIRD

Produced by Adidas, the third kit for 2011-12 was an attractive strip which - in terms of colour if not design - harked back to the club's first ever home colours before red was introduced.

THE CLUB'S FIRST COLOURS

The 2011-12 third kit consisted of a white shirt with cyan (bright blue) and black trimmings. Cyan was used for the name of sponsors Standard Chartered and featured as the colour of the usual Adidas shoulder stripes as well as the border of the sleeves, which also included a thin black line. Cyan and black also combined in a double diagonal stripe that linked the black collar with the armpit of the right-hand side. On the opposite side of the shirt was a black and red club badge with a blue Adidas logo positioned centrally, just underneath the collar. There was a break in the sleeve stripes to allow for the competition badges. Black was also used for the name and number on the back of the shirt.

This shirt was paired with white shorts, while the socks were white with a broad black and cyan hoop two-thirds of the way up and three cyan hoops on the tops. Occasionally black shorts were worn as an alternative. A similar shade of cyan/electric blue had been used on the sleeves and collar of the club's away kit in 1923-24 but otherwise this colour had not been used within the Liverpool kit since the original home colours and, as of 2022, has not been seen since. This was the last season (to 2022) that Adidas created kits for Liverpool and it was an attractive strip with a historical story with which to sign off.

There was a trophy to celebrate – but not much else. The trophy was the League Cup, edged on penalties over Cardiff City. The Wembley final saw a goal from Martin Škrtel help Liverpool come from behind to take the game into extra-time. When Dirk Kuyt then gave the Reds the lead it looked like Liverpool would have the experience and game management to see out the 12 minutes that were left, but with two minutes still to play centre-back Ben Turner forced the game to penalties.

Steven Gerrard missed Liverpool's opening spot-kick but still lifted the trophy when his cousin Anthony Gerrard missed the Bluebirds' final penalty as Kenny Dalglish's team won 3-2. It was the club's first trophy in six years, but it was not enough to save Dalglish's job. He was sacked at the end of the season despite another trip to Wembley, where this time King Kenny's side lost 2-1 in the FA Cup final to Chelsea.

With no European football Liverpool had fewer distractions in mounting their Premier League campaign, but it proved to be a very disappointing season. Only in 1993-94 had the club finished as low as eighth since the start of the Premier League but that was where they finished again in this term; only goal difference enabling them to finish above ninth-placed Fulham.

The joint-lowest number of home wins and the highest number of away defeats in the top ten was not a good combination. A paltry 24 goals scored at home in the Premier League was fewer than half what the top two Manchester clubs managed. Away from home only the top three won more than Liverpool, but equally Liverpool lost as many on the road as bottom of the table Wolves. Only in a goalless game at Wigan did Liverpool draw away from home but at Anfield nine of the 19 fixtures were drawn, more than anyone in the division.

Incredibly, in the final analysis Dalglish's side were 37 points behind champions Manchester City and only 16 ahead of relegated Bolton Wanderers.

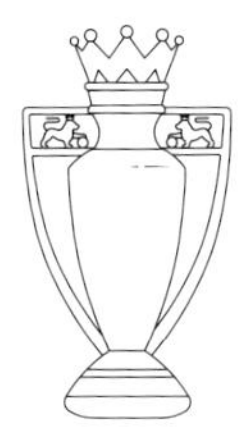

8TH

There were as many games lost as won in the Premier League.

RUNNERS-UP

Liverpool reached the FA Cup final having been drawn at home in every round up to the neutral semi-final and final.

WINNERS

Liverpool won the League Cup having only had one of the semi-final legs at home.

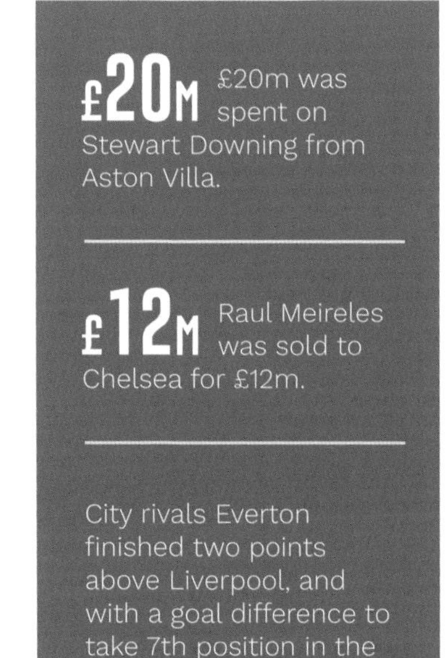

£20M £20m was spent on Stewart Downing from Aston Villa.

£12M Raul Meireles was sold to Chelsea for £12m.

City rivals Everton finished two points above Liverpool, and with a goal difference to take 7th position in the league.

7 Craig Bellamy's seven assists made him chief creator.

More Premier League games were won away from home than at Anfield.

AVERAGE HOME LEAGUE ATTENDANCE

44,253

HIGHEST ATTENDANCE

45,065

VS MANCHESTER UNITED

LOWEST ATTENDANCE

40,106

VS FULHAM

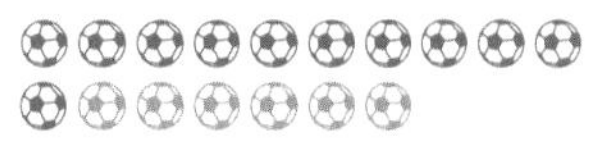

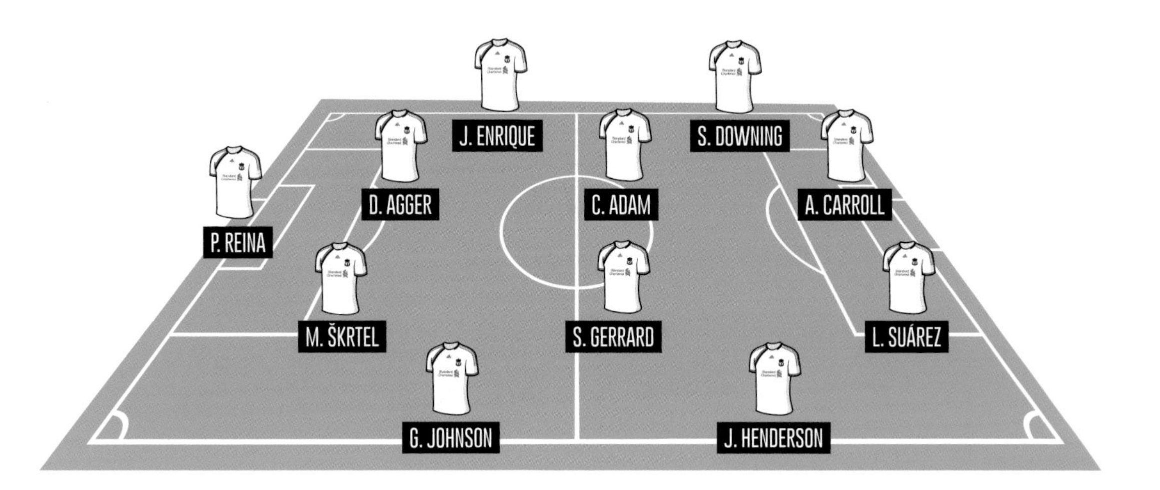

2018-19 THIRD

Made by New Balance, the third kit for 2018-19 was a two tone grey with red used for the manufacturer's logo, Standard Chartered shirt sponsorship and a slimmed down club badge featuring only the liver bird and the letters L.F.C.

EIGHTIES GREY REWORK

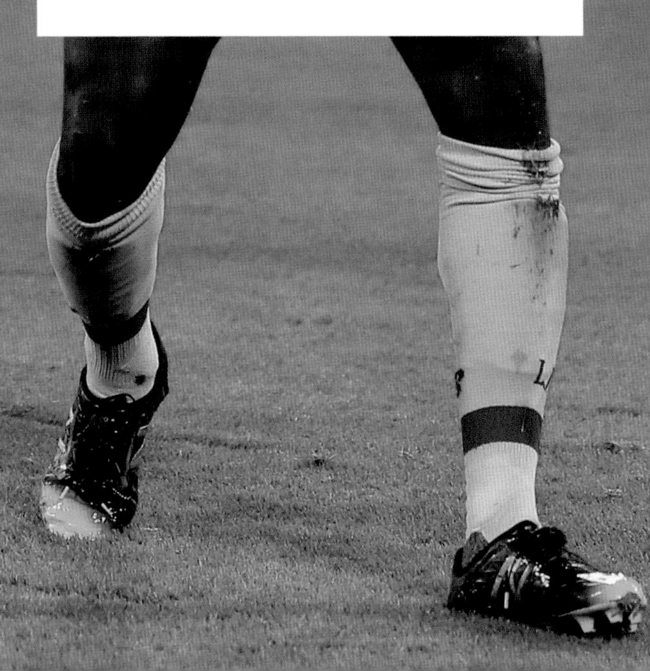

On the back of the shirt red was also used for the player name and number as well as sleeve sponsorship and a small 'Justice for the 96' logo under the collar. Grey was also the colour of the socks and shorts with the socks having a red hoop accompanied by the letters L.F.C. just above the ankle.

The shirt featured what was described as a grey violet body with a steel gradient print. It was promoted as paying tribute to kits of the 1987-91 era especially Kenny Dalglish's 1989-90 League Title winning campaign, those kits being Adidas kits.

Although the strip looked to the past its launch was very much futuristic as it was revealed in an exclusive preview of Pro Evo 19 footage of the team wearing the kit. This reportedly made Liverpool the first club to unveil a new outfit via the medium of PES video game graphics.

Jürgen Klopp inspired Liverpool to a season of glory. Having lost the previous season's Champions League final the Reds stormed back to take the trophy for a sixth time. But for the brilliance of Manchester City it would have been a double of Champions and Premier Leagues especially as Liverpool led the league for most of the season. Astonishingly Liverpool accrued 97 points having won 30, drawn seven and lost just one of their 38 fixtures. Only City in this season and the one before had ever managed more Premier League points but still the Holy Grail of the Premier League Title eluded Liverpool. Under Klopp that glory was only 12 months away.

Nonetheless 2018-19 was still a wonderful season as the Champions League came to Anfield for the first time since that iconic night in Istanbul in 2005. The group stage was one of the most difficult elements of the European win. Half of the six group games were lost as Liverpool qualified above Napoli only on goals scored having finished level on points and goal difference. A 1-0 win over the Italians in the final match securing passage to the knock out phase.

Held at home by Bayern Munich in the round of 16 Klopp's men produced a performance worthy of champions in his homeland, where two goals by Sadio Mané were the difference in a sensational 3-1 win. In contrast the quarter-final was plain sailing as Porto were beaten 2-0 on Merseyside and 4-1 on their own patch. If the quarter-final had been a breeze the semi-final was a whirlwind. Former hero Luis Suárez opened the scoring for Barcelona in the Nou Camp before two late Lionel Messi goals left Liverpool contemplating elimination as they lost the first leg 3-0.

Cue arguably the greatest of all the great Anfield European nights. Since 1986 when Barcelona themselves had come back from a three-goal deficit to beat Göteborg, no side had ever overturned a three goal mountain in the semi-final. Divock Origi got a very early goal to build hopes but Barcelona's experience and class saw them reach half time still with a two-goal cushion. Almost 10 minutes of the second half had elapsed when Barca felt the force of Klopp's Kop backed Reds. In the space of just 122 seconds Georginio Wijnaldum scored twice to sensationally bring the scores level as Barcelona's defence melted away. There could only be one winner and with 11 minutes to go Origi was on hand to net his second of the game and complete the most fantastic come-back.

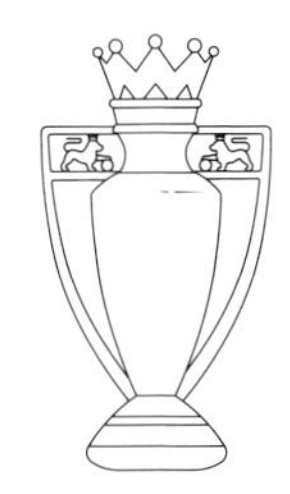

RUNNERS-UP

97 points was the third highest in top flight history.

3RD ROUND

2-1 defeat to Wolverhampton.

3RD ROUND

2-1 defeat to Chelsea.

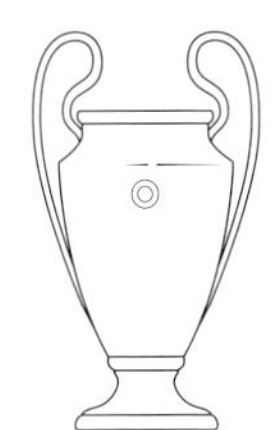

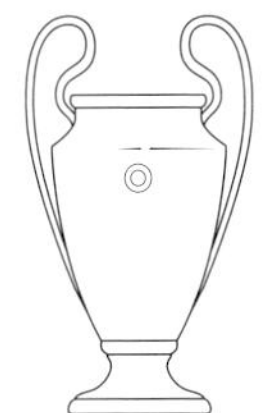

WINNERS

Liverpool won Europe's top trophy for the sixth time.

22 Sadio Mané equalled Mo Salah's total of 22 Premier League goals.

30 Premier League wins in a season equalled the club record.

Liverpool were unbeaten at Anfield for a second successive season.

4-0 The 4-0 semi-final second leg win over Barcelona was the first time any team had overturned a 3-0 semi-final first leg deficit in the Champions League era.

At The Best FIFA Football Awards, Van Dijk and Alisson were named in the FIFA FIFPro Men's World XI.

Jürgen Klopp being named as The Best FIFA Men's Coach.

JÜRGEN KLOPP

MO SALAH

AVERAGE HOME LEAGUE ATTENDANCE

52,983

HIGHEST ATTENDANCE

53,373

VS CARDIFF CITY

LOWEST ATTENDANCE

50,965

VS SOUTHAMPTON

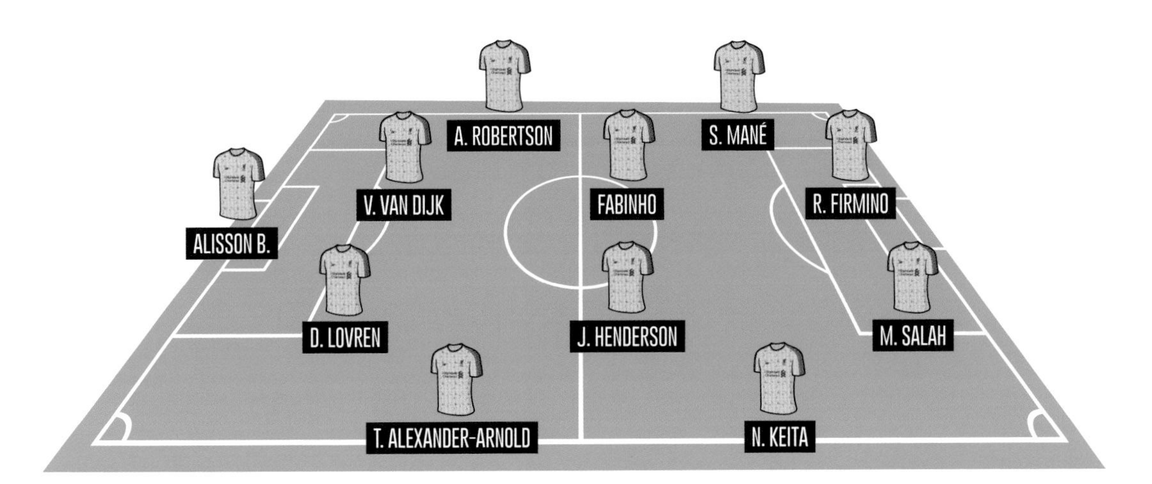

2019-20 THIRD

On a shirt described as phantom black the club crest was a nice turquoise – or vibrant Tidepool in marketing speak. It was an appropriate colour as it was meant to represent the actual colour of the liver birds from the Royal Liver building. Another Liverpool legend in Bob Paisley would have turned 100 during this season and in tribute all three of Liverpool's kits for the season included the North-Easterner's signature inside the neck of the shirt. A further detail not immediately obvious but a good idea in the eye of the designers was that a graphic on the front of the shirt was meant to be indicative of the shape of street signs used in Liverpool.

SLICK IN PHANTOM BLACK

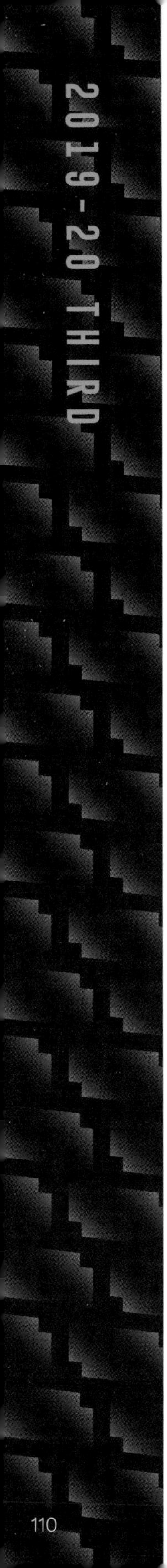

"It's always special to pull on the Liverpool shirt. The fact this one is a celebration of my city and the streets I grew up playing in makes it even better" said Merseysider Trent Alexander-Arnold loyally. A more poignant detail was the emblem commemorating the 96 (later to become 97) fans who died at Hillsborough surrounded by eternal flames. The main shirt sponsor Standard Chartered and sleeve sponsor Western Union had their names picked out in white. Completed with shorts and socks in the same phantom black with vibrant Tidepool trimmings it was an attractive kit to look at but as with all dark kits not the easiest to play in in terms of split second teammate recognition in fast paced matches.

It was a season of firsts. Not only was the Premier League finally lifted for the first time but so was the FIFA Club World Cup, and with it Liverpool became the first English club to have won the Club World Cup, Super Cup and Champions League. Having missed out on the league by one point the previous year Liverpool stormed to the title this time, defending champions Manchester City finishing 18 points behind. Premier League records were set with most wins (32), most home wins (18) and most successive victories (18).

It was a parade to the Premier League Title. A draw at Manchester United in the ninth game of the season incredibly was the only game of the first 27 that wasn't won. Defeat when it came was a shock 3-0 defeat at Watford and there was a 4-0 reverse at Manchester City who had been beaten 3-1 at Anfield. However over the marathon of the season as a whole Liverpool were so good they clinched the title with a magnificent seven games to spare – another Premier League first.

Playing in Qatar the Club World Cup was won with wins over Monterrey of Mexico and Flamengo of Brazil – Brazilian Roberto Firmino getting the winners in both games. Chelsea had been beaten on penalties in Istanbul in the Super Cup. Having won the Champions League to qualify for the Super Cup, Liverpool of course wanted to win it again but came unstuck in the quarter-finals, losing both legs to Atlético Madrid. The second leg at Liverpool came just before the shut-down of football and almost everything else due to the Covid-19 pandemic.

Over three months passed between that visit of Atlético and the resumption of the Premier League in the strange surroundings of an empty Goodison Park, as for the final nine matches of the season games were played without fans. When the time came for Sir Kenny Dalglish to present Jordan Henderson with the Premier League trophy he did so on the Kop itself. The families of the players had been given special permission to attend a game in which Chelsea were beaten 5-3. Although no fans were allowed, 'You'll Never Walk Alone' was still heard as the players sang the club's anthem themselves. Liverpool had been calling the tune all year.

WINNERS

Liverpool won the Premier League for the first time.

5TH ROUND

2-0 defeat to Chelsea.

QTR-FINALS

5-0 win for Aston Villa.

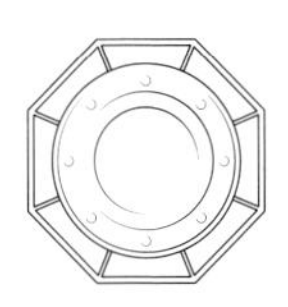

RUNNERS-UP

Losing on penalties to Manchester City.

WINNERS

The Club World Cup was won for the first time.

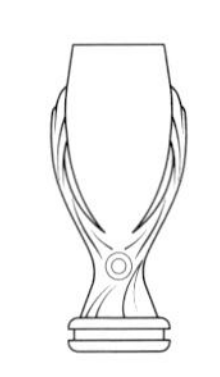

WINNERS

The UEFA Super Cup was won on penalties against Chelsea.

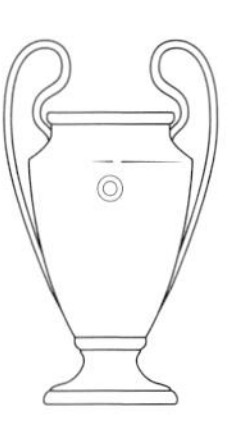

LAST 16

140,000 fans from both clubs traveled to the final, with only 16,000 fans from each club getting tickets!

It was the club's 19th League Title.

The season was suspended from the 5th of April to the 17th of June due to Covid 19. The final game of the Premier League season was not until 26th July.

AVERAGE HOME LEAGUE ATTENDANCE

53,143

based on games where spectators were allowed

HIGHEST ATTENDANCE

53,333 VS NORWICH CITY

LOWEST ATTENDANCE

51,430 VS NEWCASTLE UNITED

Four home games had no spectators due to Covid restrictions

JÜRGEN KLOPP

MO SALAH

LIVERPOOL

CLASSIC KITS

Written by Rob Mason
Designed by Daniel Brawn

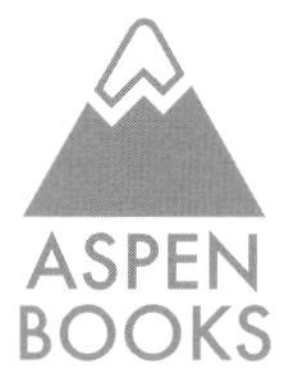

This is an independent publication. It has no connection with Liverpool Football Club or with any organisation or individual connected in any way whatsoever with Liverpool Football Club.

Any quotes within this publication which are attributed to anyone connected to Liverpool Football Club have been sourced from other publications, or from the internet and, as such, are a matter of public record.

Whilst every effort has been made to ensure the accuracy of information within this publication, the publisher shall have no liability to any person or entity with respect to any inaccuracy, misleading information, loss or damage caused directly or indirectly by the information contained within this book.

ISBN: 978-1-914536-27-4